Guide
Yourself
through
Old Age

Guide Yourself through Old Age

OREN ARNOLD

FORTRESS PRESS   Philadelphia

Library of Congress Catalog Card Number 76–9712
ISBN 0–8006–1239–6

5767E76   Printed in U.S.A.   1–1239

As for old age, embrace it and love it. It abounds with pleasure, if you know how to use it. The gradually (I do not say rapidly) declining years are amongst the sweetest in a person's life; and I maintain that even where they have reached the extreme limit, they have their pleasure still.

—Seneca

Contents

Preface

Old people do not need or want a lot of pampering. We freeze up against unctuous preachments or moralizations.

We have intelligence—more than the average youngster ever suspects!—and generally we have very high ideals.

On the other hand, we are slightly more frail than we were, say, forty years ago, more susceptible to physical and emotional strains. And here lately, due to the accelerating rate of technological and social change, the *newness* all around us and increasing by the hour, we have found ourselves confused.

We do not care to read thick think-tomes on "gerontology" and such; let the professors and other academicians blow the big winds of theory. What interests us is some short, specific what-to/how-to aid in adjusting to our remaining years on earth. There are millions and millions of us over the age of sixty now, and it is fair to guess that at least 98 percent of us—maybe 99 percent—are worried in some degree about old age.

The sole purpose of this book is to alleviate that worry. The specifics are here, with no circumlocution, no maudlin sentimentality. I have used straight talk, commonsense counsel based on the vast stores of knowledge now available to us. Also I have tested the manuscript on enough old folk to know that such a techique is appreciated and helpful. If I seem a little blunt at times, do not take offense; weigh the matter carefully in your mind.

Whoever you are, wherever you are, I wish you well.

O. A.

Acknowledgments

Hundreds of persons graciously helped in the research for this book and in testing the manuscript. Personal interviews were conducted with aging folk at all levels, in and out of "retirement centers." In addition, the findings and data of specialists and research agencies were studied and correlated with the author's own interviews.

Among the many individuals who were most helpful are Karl Menninger, renowned octogenarian psychiatrist; George W. Crane and William Bede McGrath, distinguished psychiatrists and psychologists; Ben Pat Frissell and Thaddeus C. Jones, medical doctors; Ross Cortese, founder and still manager of the astonishingly successful Leisure World towns; Albert O. Hjerpe and Norman Vincent Peale, ministers; G. Barter Bell, Bessie A. Bell, and Ruth Lindstrom, retirement specialists in Scottsdale House, Arizona, and in Hudson, Wisconsin; Opal Preston of Henderson, Texas; Sylvester and Lucille Hall and Mary Lou Miller of Laguna Hills, California.

Fourteen major agencies for studying the problems of aging persons were consulted, including such outstanding ones as the Ethel Percy Andrus Gerontology

Center, University of Southern California; SERVE (Serve and Enrich Retirement) of New York City; Duke University's Center for the Study of Aging; the Commission on Aging, Richmond, Indiana; and Reports of the White House Conference on Aging.

The author is grateful to all these unofficial collaborators.

I.

Face This First–And Have Done with It!

Years ago a famous young whippersnapper named Thoreau said, "The mass of men lead lives of quiet desperation."

He was wrong.

Conceivably he was a genius in some areas, but he didn't really know people. Or he would have known that all truly God-loving folk live lives of zestful *inspiration*.

They live that way constantly, as long as they stay on earth. And have firm assurance that it will continue even after that, forever.

⟦About Yourself Now–⟧

How about you? Are you going to be one of the miserable minority who *fight* old age? In a welter of self-pity, will you allow your last years to be a period of gloom and doom?

Or maybe it's fear that rides you. Fear!

The happy majority knows little of fear. They know —and you can know—that the only fear we ever need to worry about is the fear of God's displeasure.

⟦Antidote to Fear⟧

The ungodly man or woman invariably is afraid of

1

dying. We see them by the thousands—doddery, trembly, scared old folk, well aware that they have little time left. Or a few who, in pitiable and obvious straining, try in public to act defiant.

You do not have to join either group. There is a positive antidote to the fear, a spiritual vaccination, an absolute preventive.

It is *faith!*

Faith in what? In whom?

You have to figure that out for yourself. It is extremely important, but also very personal.

Truly, many old people face death placidly, while many others show an almost panicky fear of it. You must ask yourself—why is that?

Fear of punishment for our sins could make anybody panicky, and people have known this at least since the time of Christ. But the matter is a bit more complicated than that. A recent and highly interesting discovery has been made by psychologists, notably Lisl Marburg Goodman of Jersey City State College. She (and others) have said that fear of death is linked in intricate ways with *creativity*.

Tightening it, Mrs. Goodman said, "The more complete one's life is, the more one's destiny and one's creative capacities are fulfilled, *the less one fears death*. People are seldom afraid of death per se, but of the incompleteness of their lives."

How about that! Startling, isn't it? Food for thought, surely.

Translated, it seems to mean that if we just sit there and wail and worry and do nothing good (or creative) we are out of luck; we shall certainly face death with panicky fear. Faith in God and in oneself is a first requirement for any creative effort. Which rather catches the cynics up short, doesn't it?

IF NECESSARY REORIENT YOUR THINKING

It is highly unlikely that you are atheistic. Studies show that among 10,000 oldsters there is fewer than one real atheist.

Atheism is a passing disease of the mind. Sometimes it temporarily strikes young folk, and even a few older ones who remain mentally immature. Some people proclaim it to get attention, feeling unable to build up their status in a more valid way. But even primitive peoples know better.

Proclaiming yourself an atheist is the most colossal of all conceits. You are saying that you are wiser than virtually all the presidents, kings, and queens, wiser than most of the philosophers and other intellectuals, most of the great scientists, industrial leaders, and statesmen, the truly gifted and creative folk at all levels, and wiser indeed than 90 percent of the humbler people on earth. Positive faith in God is humanity's greatest undergirding. Without it, a form of madness soon arises.

Thus to the genuine believers, who "put on the whole armor" of God, death is not much more of a transition than moving from some cold and smoky city to sunshiny, flower-decked Miami or San Diego. It means a reunion with loved ones, and offers a glory far beyond anything our mortal minds can conceive. The promise is not mine; it is God's.

So—

3

Make Your "Arrangements" Then Refocus Your Mind

If you haven't already done so, then right now, today, *write down* any instructions to your survivors. What shall be done with what is generally called your "remains"?

Come to think on it—what do you care? Why be concerned with what happens to them?

Such a disinterested, disdainful attitude is by no means a bad one. Wherefore, you might well tell your survivors to do whatever they please. Do suggest, however, that they make up their minds in advance, to avoid emotional conflicts.

But for thousands of years, people *have* cared about the disposal of their bodies. They have made themselves almost comical in their preoccupation with preserving them—as witness all those tombs in the Pyramids and elsewhere B.C. But don't smirk. Consider also how we modern, enlightened, faith-proclaiming folk here in the late twentieth century A.D. still waste millions of dollars a year trying to box the body permanently after having it embalmed. Very commonly, we enlightened people even specify this foolishness in our wills.

Why do we do this?

We are told on absolute authority, and by common sense, that "preserving the body" is a delusion.

So, in cold intelligent reasoning we have to ask ourselves, "What body? As of what date?" Because the truth is, the body you inhabit right this moment, is completely different from the one you inhabited even last year! Medical science now tells us that *every cell*

4

in the human body is replaced by a new one every 120 days! (So says Professor Marcel Bessis at the Institute of Cellular Pathology in Paris). Hence the physical you of today is certainly not the same you that walked the earth in 1920 or even 1970. We cannot allow ourselves to be in love with our physical bodies. Yes, while we are on earth and need them, we are obligated to take the best possible care of them. But after that, they will disintegrate into literal dust or soil, all in a split second as God measures time.

Personally, I opt for cremation.

With no costly casket, no embalming, no cemetery plot, no urn to sit on a mantle for my heirs to get maudlin about—or smile at! Cremation can be very inexpensive; burial can run into the thousands, and that money could be far better spent on some worthy charity.

But if this kind of truthful talk causes your hackles to rise—I will give in, I will still love you, I will in fact be one of your pallbearers if I am asked to, and tote you expensively to your grave. But I will know that I'm not carrying the real *you*. Resurrection? Yes, of course I believe in it. The really genuine you, to be resurrected, is your spirit. So refocus your attention outward, and upward. You have a lot of joyous living yet to do, old friend.

Just make whatever "arrangements" you wish to—at once. Then the matter need never haunt you again.

Now let's move on.

2.

This Horrid
Younger Generation!

As I have just reminded you, your awareness of approaching death is the top-priority item in your consciousness. And I showed you how to cope with that.

Your second concern is more fun!

The authorities all agree (and my own studies verify it) that the second most prevalent matter in the minds of us old people is the *young* folk around us.

We tend to behold them with something akin to consternation. And perhaps not totally without cause—heavens, just look at them! And listen to them!

And yet, something inside us warns us not to judge them too hastily. Their time on earth is not our time, so to speak. And while the eternal verities remain fixed forever, the stimuli and excitements and mores and manners do not.

The old have always been concerned with the young, of course. We have written proof of it, dating far back before the time of Christ. But it is probable that the concern today is greater than ever before, largely because modern news media keep us better informed on what the young are doing. This has made many of us with bald heads or gray hair and wrinkled skins and brown spots on our hands and arthritic joints and atrophied attitudes, horrified.

Wherefore, let us formally open the meeting here by stating some of the more tragic and oft-heard premises:

1. Our own children have grown away from us; they no longer really care what becomes of us.

2. Life is very hard on old people, because children neglect them.

3. We scrimped and sacrificed to give our children every advantage we could, and what thanks do we get now? They barely know we exist.

4. This younger generation is wild and sinful. They have forgotten God.

5. Just look at the licentiousness, flaunting of sex, thievery, flippant attitudes.

6. It shows in everything they do. For instance, how can they possibly call their modern phonograph and radio noises "music"?

7. And look at their clothing! I tell you, my mother would turn over in her grave.

8. Modern youth is destroying our country. Only this morning, I read in the paper where police are saying that there is more crime and violence than ever before in history.

We could go and on; such lamentations of the elderly are endless. Not *all* the elderly, of course; many do not talk in that vein at all, and it is to be hoped that you are one who doesn't.

As for the ones who do—it is necessary now to disillusion them, by direct contradiction. In the process, perhaps we can help also to tighten down your own instincts into sharp words for use as needed.

7

Let us now relook at those eight common premises, and see if there is any way we can comfort ourselves.

1. *"Our children have grown away from us."*

It is probable that Adam and Eve first said that. Some of their children were inconsiderate, recalcitrant, reprehensible. One was even a murderer. Very likely, too, when Mr. and Mrs. Noah re-established residence on solid earth, their kids began to kick over the traces, going about their own exciting new interests and tending to forget the old folks still in their rocking chairs back yonder on the deck of the ark. The pattern has continued through the centuries.

So there is ample precedent. Hence it may indeed be true that your children have grown away from you. But if so—who is to blame?

Actually, assessing blame is always the most futile of human endeavors, no matter what the situation. A better approach is to accept the current situation and build anew around that.

If—*if*, mind you—your children are truly neglecting you, then you must not just sit and mope about it. Self-pity is always a cancer on the soul; you will get no real comfort from it, but only a kind of narcotic postponement of the inevitable. So if you truly cannot get needed, wanted help and love from your children, grown or otherwise, then *shrug the matter off*. Accept the truth. And start immediately to build your last years without them.

⟦ WHERE TO GET HELP ⟧

Go to your pastor or rabbi for quiet counsel in the

matter. (If you don't have one, it's high time you did! But regardless of that, even clergy that may be strangers to you will be anxious to help you wherever they can. That's their calling in life.)

Make no bitter accusations, mind you; this would do no good at all. Just make a calm statement of fact, and a request for guidance in your particular case. It will be held in strict confidence. The "talking it out" will bring initial relief; as you empty your reservoir of despair, your soul becomes receptive to something much better.

Most likely the pastoral counselor will help you reorient your physical and emotional life. In rare instances legal action may be suggested, to force some well-to-do son or daughter to help bear the burden of your living costs. If so, take the action. If in your old-age incapacities you happen to be dependent and you have children who could pay your bills, see to it that they do so. Turn the matter over to an honest attorney, and go on from that point.

I repeat—do not mope, whine, or cry. Do not nurse bitterness. Do not assess blame, on them or on yourself. Do take action, for in that lies the only comfort you are going to get.

2. "Life is very hard on old people, because children neglect us."

Not so. Life is hard on you because of your own shortcomings. Over the years, you were careless, or wasteful, or inept—if we *must* assess blame!

Truth is, life is hard on young people too, my friend. Young folk have their weaknesses, their illnesses, their

9

doubts and insecurity feelings, their financial and social problems, their worries and fears. Many are worse off than we oldsters are because they do not have the wisdom born of experience that you and I can claim. Most of us can well remember hard times, notably the financial depression of 1930–40. Our big children tend to think that the affluent society is a standard condition, hence are appalled and bewildered by its handmaiden, inflation. In 1930, you and I learned how to "do without." Our heirs today tend to think that luxury living is theirs by divine right.

⟦ YOU MUST STILL PADDLE YOUR OWN CANOE ⟧

Generally, you and I have learned to weigh real values more appreciatively. We can see goodness where the younger folk can't. In sacrifice, for instance. In the ability to make do with less. Your 1970s grandson may be "hurt" if he doesn't get at least $100 worth of toys and luxuries for Christmas, whereas you and I probably were happier with just a two-dollar popgun and an orange in the toe of our stocking. Truly, "we the people" have been trapped into putting high value on physical things, rather than on spiritual grandeur. The result is a sociological confusion.

With all of that alibiing, statistics definitely prove that most children do *not* neglect their parents; the parents just think they do.

Most children love their elders. Regrettably, and unnecessarily, we elders, in a selfish reach for sympathy, often tend to become too demanding. In our old age, we want to become *leaners*.

But harken to this overriding fact:

As long as you and I are physically and mentally able to do so, we must paddle our own canoes. We have the moral obligation to take care of ourselves and not be dependent.

"But I slaved and sacrificed and did everything for my kids when they were young!" you may shout back indignantly. "The least they can do now is take care of me."

Don't be stupid, friend. That has been the pleasure pattern for parents since the day of Adam and Eve—loving and taking care of kids. Your parents did it for you. You did it for yours. The pattern is passed on from generation to generation. If you loved and helped your young ones selfishly, just so you could sponge on them later—shame on you. Inevitably, they will have sensed your hypocrisy, and feel cool toward you now.

Nobody really "owes" us support. Every couple is expected to make their own way on earth, honorably and proudly—every individual if you live alone. Unless you accept that dictum of dignity, you are likely to become a crotchety old coot or old biddy whom nobody can love.

The best approach is to *ask the children themselves* for guidance when needed. Discuss your arising problems with them openly, lovingly, and with good humor all around. Almost certainly a "miracle" will develop, guaranteeing you an abiding peace of mind.

3. *"We scrimped and saved" and all that.*

So you did. Back yonder, you scrimped and saved. But see here, Buster and Bertha, most likely it was because you had to! Honest now—wasn't it? You folk, and my Adele and I, were no more noble in our young-married years than our married children are in theirs. Life repeats, you know.

If you truly scrimped and saved to help your children, you can be sure that the children know about it. Probably the reason they "don't know you exist" now—if they don't, which I doubt—is that you harp on it. You did your duty back there in your young years. So make a selfless and sensible approach now, and chances are they will do theirs.

4. "This younger generation is wild and sinful. Its members have forgotten God."

Maybe they never knew God. Did you introduce him to them?

Regardless, the lamentation is a common one. But don't you believe it! No such critical, condemning, pessimistic generality has any merit, because the facts simply do not bear it out.

The fact is, more young people are engaged in religious worship today than ever before in history—though not always in the conventional Gothic-arch church that you and I know.

The further absolute fact is, more books on religion are being sold today than ever before in history, and mostly to young people. That includes many wonderful new editions of the Bible, but also many inspiriting, helpful commentaries thereon.

Psychologically your lamentation about "wild and sinful" youth stems primarily from an unrecognized, unadmitted envy, the experts say.

Yes, envy!

In those young rascals ten to twenty-five or so, turning cartwheels and leaping tennis nets and *vrrrooming* their motors and eating everything available and giggling and swimming and slamming doors in a devil-may-care manner and kissing one another and dressing slouchily and generally flaunting conventions, we see ourselves as—let's face it—we used to be, and would like to be again. Any time we deny it, we are likely to end up being sanctimonious or senile. Hoo boy, I can well remember what a problem *I* was, back there around World War I time! My parents despaired. How I did love to show off for pretty Bonny Flanagan and Sarah Compton, galloping around on my Shetland pony! How I loved to nag and tease my old-maidish teachers, male and female! How skillful I was at avoiding work chores at home! What supreme contempt I nursed for almost anybody over twenty-one years of age! Them was, indeed, the good old days.

All right, be tolerant now. Youth today *seems* wild and ungodly. (Once I put a live frog under our pastor's pulpit Bible shortly before morning service). Actually, youth today is reaching, just as we were. Asserting itself, reaching for excellence. Searching, yearning for godliness as probably no other generation has ever done. They have more reason to, more awareness of need; they are at least twice as intelligent as we were in the 1920s. Which is a *good* something, isn't it?

LOVE AND GUIDANCE, NOT BLANKET CONDEMNATION

Back there, our glands were developing and "acting

13

up," just as the inherited glands are in today's youths. Adrenaline still flows, and the hyperkinetic kid is still a home-and-town problem. But the very same kids also are growing spiritually, maturing in soul; they merit our love and guidance, not our blanket condemnation.

Ask Billy Graham (as I have). That great evangelist can fill a stadium with young folk wherever he goes, and when he invites them to give their hearts to God they come streaming by the thousands. If the church building, the Bible school, the worship service, and other religious routines that *we* grew up under seem not to captivate today's youth, perhaps we need to re-inspect and upgrade our own dissemination of god-liness. We cannot live in the past.

5. *"But look at all the licentiousness, sex, thievery."*

True, true, some youths in the area engaged in illicit sex last night. Some stole hubcaps yesterday, broke a few windows, sassed a few professors, all that.

But for every such rebellious youth in your town last night or yesterday, at least 10,000 more were at home helping Mom with the dishes, doing their school-work, mowing the lawn, washing the car, ticking the dog, playing catch with little brother, enjoying the home hi-fi, doing their hair, living normal youthful lives with absolutely no need of attention from the public or the police.

That is not merely a fatuously optimistic theory of mine; it is a cold, statistical fact.

Far fewer than 1 percent of the people under the age of twenty-five, the sociologists tell us, are responsible for all the noisy misconduct that makes the headlines and the town talk. Pressed, even the police will admit it, and so will the clergy.

When you and I view with alarm, friends, could it be that we are simply getting old? And half-blind, sociologically? And intolerant? Let's stop condemning the few troublesome youth who make all those lurid headlines and scandalous talk, and start encouraging them to emulate the lovable majority. Creating ways to do that can become your most rewarding old-age adventure.

6. *"It shows in everything they do. For instance, their music . . . ."*

Hah, I see eye to eye with you there! More exactly, ear to ear. Their "rock" records are awful, aren't they? A cacophony of drums, a blaring of brass, an absence of melody, accompanied by an insane swaying of shoulders and flailing of arms. There ought to be a law!

All right, I recall that my Mama—rest her soul—figured that I was going to hell because I belted out "Alexander's Ragtime Band" back in the early 1900s, then compounded the felony by sneering a little, snapping my fingers with Bonny and Eva Jo and singing "Everybody's doin' it, doin' it. . . ." How sinful we were! Mama and the good Reverend Brother Hornbeak prayed for our redemption.

Let the kids today have their living room, and do not butt in on them. Make them feel welcome in their own homes, and in ours. Let them use the silly records they enjoy. You and I can go over to the local recreation center or to the homes of our aging friends and

15

put on some records that have Nelson Eddy singing "Indian Love Call" to Jeanette MacDonald. And on the way home under the moonlight we two old folk can softly sing "Ay, 'tis love and love alone the world is seek-ing. . . ." Which is a statement of fact.

And you know something? Those noisy kids love us. They really do.

7. *"Just look at their costumes!"*

I doubt if my father ever saw my mother's legs (pardon me, *limbs!*) above her shoe tops. In the fashion of her day, her stupid dresses over myriad petticoats literally dragged the floor and grass and dirt.

Even in college at Rice University, where I fancied myself the fair-haired sophisticate, and got myself elected editor of the weekly newspaper, and roomed with the cheerleader, and sashayed around with dozens of co-eds, and married up with one of them (the prettiest one) I wore an absolutely horrid white collar three inches high and stiff as steel, held onto a narrow shirt band with poke-in buttons that eternally got lost. And the girl I married was, forsooth, a "flapper." Meaning that she had a horribly shapeless dress with waistline down below the hips—the ugliest creation ever known in feminine attire. It was worse than my peg-topped pants, and my later zoot suit.

Ah, well. In every degeneration a few young folk sink low, but their number is always minimal. They are not a national calamity. And don't glare sanctimoniously at me when I say that I rather like today's mini-bra and string bikini seen at the beach where I

16

live. One of the twenty-two-year-old "regulars" there sings in our choir too.

I often wonder if my mother had a beautiful, God-given body.

8. *"Youth is destroying our country. There is more crime and violence than ever before."*

Oh-oh, here we go again! I thought we had cleared up this matter back there in Item No. 5.

So I repeat—such calamity howlers are in error.

They have viewed with alarm so assiduously that they have lost their vision.

Millions of good but fearful, faithless folk—notably among us elders—join them in their propaganda of doom, reiterating ad nauseam what they consider to be fact—that youth has pushed crime in general to an all-time high.

But the cold truth is, in percentage there is far *less* crime and violence today than ever before in our history. The most authoritative estimates run from 40 to 70 percent less.

Shocking to you, isn't it! How can anyone say that? You are indignant. Naturally. Because you read the papers every day, and you listen to earnest newscasts on your TV, and you listen to your minister. You keep yourself informed!

〚 JUST CALM DOWN NOW
AND LISTEN TO REASON 〛

At this point in your reading, put the book down, go get a drink of water, eat two or three cookies, inhale deeply a few times, look out the window, relax, and generally get a grip on yourself so that you can come back here with an open mind.

Let us proceed:

The cold truth again is—in *percentage*, I said. There is more *total* outlawry. But there is more total of everything, including people and houses and cars and cities and buttons and handkerchiefs and toothpicks. Their increase has been astronomical. Hence it would be astounding if we did not have a volume increase in badness as well as goodness.

For proof that the *percentage* is down—the total crime in proportion to the total number of people—we have only to look at history.

Life in Elizabethan England—the nation which really begat us—was little short of hellish. Constant crime and violence were an accepted way of life, this despite many public hangings with the corpses left dangling at roadside corners for weeks, and despite many lifetime sentences served in prisons that were horrifying. In that era every traveler needed armed escort, highwaymen and muggers were rampant, all doors and windows had to be barred and locked at night, just walking any street was exceedingly dangerous. Her majesty was at wit's end to find any corrective measures.

In the colonies a blunderbuss, a dagger, a sword, even a hand ax, were literally necessities of life for anyone venturing more than a few yards from his cabin. This was true all through the Revolutionary period. In the time of Washington and Jefferson, crime on the city streets—day and night—was exceeded only by dishonesty and graft in high places. Watergate was

18

trivial compared to the political chicanery of those days.

In that era, too, outlawry on country roads was unbelievable. Most of the citizens could neither read nor write, hence could not defend themselves from confidence men, grafters, slickers in general, not to mention violent highwaymen who lurked on almost every road. Women and children were frequent victims. Vandalism was routine.

This continued right on through the nineteenth century. Both North and South in mid-century were so violent that virtually every male over the age of fourteen had to carry rifle and pistol everywhere he went. Duels were common. Ambushings, fist fights, killings, drunkenness, doors and windows barred at night, the loaded rifle over the mantle, arson, the constant need for alertness and self-defense—all were accepted as inevitable. Most of the outlaws were under thirty years of age.

"But what about the authorities, the police?" you exclaim.

What police?

Police were virtually unknown, unheard of! The few "forces" that were in existence were composed of a few inept and confused and fearful men who could accomplish almost nothing. Police science had not been invented. Mob rule alone had power, and even it was sporadic and inconsistent.

After the Civil War matters were even worse. Millions moved westward, hoping not only to find gold but mostly to find a more safe and peaceful environment, a better pattern of living. What they did find in St.

Louis, Dodge City, Denver, El Paso, Santa Fe, Tombstone, Tucson, Laramie, Reno, Cheyenne, Portland, "Frisco," and in that new town ironically named "The Angels" (Los Angeles) was—

Even more vicious violence and crime! Mostly by young people.

Every man and bigger boy wore a gun, often two. Survival required it. The side arms, the quick-draw attitude, the saloon, the bawdy house, the stagecoach robberies, and the general atmosphere of outlawry so commonly portrayed on television and motion picture screen are not much exaggerated. They were a routine part of living. And yes, the older folk back there loudly lamented that the young hellions were driving the nation to the dogs.

Do You Carry a Rifle? A Pistol? A Belt Knife?

By contrast, do you carry a rifle around in your normal routine today, sir? Do you even own one? Do you wear a pistol on your thigh, a knife in your belt, a deadly little Derringer up your sleeve? Do you?

Can your wife get in her stagecoach (eight cylinders, not eight horses) and drive alone, happily, the 400 miles from Phoenix to Los Angeles with no thought of danger from criminals? My wife does that routinely, even though she has lived seventy years. A scant century ago, she would have had to have armed men escorting her as protection from young brigands.

Randy H. Hamilton and Edwin H. Pfuhl, renowned criminologists with the Institute for Local Self Government, recently finished long studies into this matter of outlawry. Sociologist-author Walter W. Meek reported on their findings: "The reputed surge of crime in recent years seems to be a myth. In fact it appears that so-called crime waves *can be created in the minds of the public by police reporting techniques.*"

That statement points a finger directly at the crux of the matter—our new, modern *awareness* of crime by young people and others. When President Lincoln was assassinated, thousands of people in the backwoods hadn't heard about it even six months later. When President Kennedy was shot, virtually every person on earth knew about it in a few hours. In 1876 a stage-coach holdup and murder might not be known in the nearest village for two weeks. Today a bank holdup is very likely to be televised even while it is in progress, as has frequently happened. Then it will be on TV and radio dozens of times before next dawn, and head-lined in thousands of newspapers and repeated in news-casts all next day.

"That's the sad part," declared Karl Menninger, the distinguished psychiatrist, one of the world's foremost authorities on this matter. "The constant reiteration of bad news, warps our thinking. We hear reports of the same crime again and again and again. The news media tell us about it so often that we can hardly focus on anything else. Our most sensible people can thus be brainwashed. Undoubtedly there is much more talk about crime than there is crime itself."

Now come the "yes buts."

We oldsters are the world's yes-buttingest bunch of citizens. We are die-hards; we have our opinions, and by gosh nobody is going to shake us out of them. "A

21

man convinced against his will, is of the same opinion still" (somebody said that years ago). *We* know what we are talking about, no matter what the authorities say.

An oft-heard one is, "Yes, but the Director of the FBI, the local police chief, and even our pastor, all say we have more crime than ever, especially among youths."

"Yes" they do, "but"—

But all three of those individuals *have a vested interest in crime.* They are professional viewers with alarm. They have to belabor us with the incessant dangers in order to get adequate appropriations to operate their offices! Had you realized that?

Oh, we might say that the clergy are at least honest about it; they think they are right. The truth is, again, that they have brainwashed themselves; they see and hear so much about sin, that they often miss the grander truth about outlawry—that its percentage is way down.

⟦ IN-DEPTH THINKING ⟧
⟦ IS CALLED FOR HERE ⟧

Crime is horrible today? Yes, dear God, it is. John F. Kennedy was assassinated, along with Robert Kennedy, Martin Luther King, Jr. More recently, demented people have threatened or tried to shoot the President. We do have to nurse all those shames.

But let us reflect once more. We recall nineteenth-century presidents who suffered from assassins. There were many threats on the life of Abraham Lincoln, so many that the Pinkerton Detective Agency had to be

22

hired to protect him, and even that ultimately failed. Grant was also on John Wilkes Booth's death list that night, but just happened to decline Mr. Lincoln's invitation to Ford Theater. We know that Garfield and McKinley were killed. Teddy Roosevelt was shot in Milwaukee. A spray of bullets hit Franklin Roosevelt's car in Miami, killing Chicago Mayor Anton Cermak and wounding four others. Harry Truman was shot at in Blair House.

So after all, the more recent attempts and assassinations do not tag our modern era as one of originality. The "politics of assassination" has been in operation at least since the time of Caesar. During the Jackson administration, Vice-President Van Buren felt it necessary while presiding over the august United States Senate itself to wear a brace of pistols under his belt. Can you imagine that being necessary in the Senate chamber today?

⟦ THE NATION HAS ALWAYS BEEN ON THE VERY BRINK OF DISASTER ⟧

Yes, something or somebody is forever out to get us, and more often than not, it is some wild bunch of younger-generation enemies. Nothing ever has brought disaster to us. Not the English, the Germans, the Italians, the Japanese, the French, the Indians, the Spanish, or the Mexicans. Not the Russians, the North Koreans, the North Vietnamese, the dishonest Democrats, the dishonest Republicans, the Arabs hoarding their oil, the atheists, the airplane hijackers, or the governmental bureaucrats. Not the atom bomb, the hydrogen bomb, poison gas, or energy shortages. After

23

all these years, here we still are, bigger, better, more prosperous, safer than ever, in spite of "all these wild young people." Perhaps the only truly classless society in the world today, we are one nation *under God*.

Throw off your worries about our young people and the nation, and sleep well tonight.

3.

Things Are Not the Same Anymore

They never were, of course. There has always been change, and you well know it. Nevertheless, the onslaught of change, of newness, ranks as a high third among the matters that disturb us oldsters. Thus we owe it to ourselves to put it on a laboratory table and dissect it.

There are many facets to this change or newness. There is physical change everywhere, certainly in our own bodies and those of our loved ones. Similarly, there is mental change, wholly new attitudes that often leave us appalled. There is political and economic and social and every other kind of change, from day to day, month to month, year to year. Newness is as inescapable as death; newness is a part of life.

But the big news of today is—even *that* has changed!
The rate of change itself has accelerated suddenly, spectacularly, powerfully, often devastatingly. But that has also brought a potentially grand, inspiriting force, a wholly new opportunity for humanity—and by all means you and I must latch onto that!

No sir, absolutely not, it is *not* good enough for you!
Our fathers had their way of life; we in turn must have
ours. And we must make ours totally new and up-
graded; otherwise there would never be any progress!

All of us oldsters have, seemingly, an inborn urge
to worship the status quo. We seem never to want
change; we continually fight it. But if we human beings
had done that right along, we would all still be carrying clubs, wearing animal skins, and living in caves.

Now, what has caused the rate of change suddenly
to accelerate in our time?

The answer is quite clear. It has been caused by the
utterly astounding sudden acceleration in the acquisition of new human knowledge. That spurt in our learning—right here in *our* lifetime—is almost unbelievable.

Scientists now tell us that human beings have been
on earth for four and one-half million years. (Until
just a few years ago, a distinguished "authority" had us
all believing that humans were created in 4200 B.C., a
scant tick of the clock compared to those millions).
During that long stretch we learned many things: how
to get food and shelter, how to start a fire, how to make
a wheel, how to catch a horse and hitch it to a wheel,
and on and on. But it all came slowly; the rate of
change was minimal.

In due time a form of "civilization" was achieved
by humankind. We became quite sophisticated, compared to the cave dwellers. Somewhere in there, the

acquisition of human knowledge began to speed up. Christianity came along, as the most revolutionary knowledge we earthlings had ever received. It too upset millions of people—you just can't imagine what a stir the Resurrection caused!

Meanwhile new weapons of war were being developed, and that has continued right down to the present. One day the Pope himself, critically disturbed by the developing military sophistication, issued a papal bull about a new weapon just invented. He said that it was so powerful, so dangerous, that its use could not be permitted because it would surely destroy humankind. And he wasn't speaking of the atom bomb, or even gunpowder. The weapon the Pope referred to in this instance was the crossbow!

We now know that the acquisition of new knowledge began to accelerate most noticeably during the Renaissance. Newness, change, became the order of the day in Europe. It must have distressed the oldsters in Elizabethan England to discover that what had been good enough for their fathers was not good enough for themselves.

Scientists and other freethinkers began to populate a New World, and we know the story of humanity from there on. The steamboat came along, then the railroad train. Franklin's electricity (a mere novelty, though dangerous) developed slowly; as late as 1880, experts said that it had no more future, it had gone as far in human use as it ever could go.

Fortunately, not everybody believed those experts. One young man lost his job because of them. So he spent $7.50 for wire and metal, and in a tiny room over a horse stable began hand-making electric motors. He peddled them house-to-house by pedaling around on a high-wheeled bicycle. From that start developed the world's largest electric welding corporation and chain of factories—the Lincoln Electric Company in Cleveland. I met that still-young genius, John C. Lincoln, in our home church when he was gray-haired and a bit stooped. He had come to Phoenix to retire and rock away his life in a rocking chair. I bawled him out about that; I told him he would become senile if he allowed his great mind to retire. Two weeks later he bestirred himself—and built one of the most beautiful, still most luxurious and appealing resort hotels in the world, famed Camelback Inn, near Phoenix. And yes, he had electric lights in it! We kidded him about that, shortly before we carried him to his grave. An "old" man, thinking and working and achieving—in fact *creating* new knowledge through experiments and inventions—right up to the week of his passing.

That same electricity, made more efficiently with new knowledge, brought us what was surely the ultimate in human communication—or so the then experts declared. That ultimate was the telegraph and the telephone. Miracles! Beyond all human anticipation or hope or dreaming.

Many people considered them sinful.

Many more considered the airplane sinful, when it came along; the Wright brothers had defied God himself! "If God had wanted people to fly, he would have given us wings." We smile at that now; back then, it was said in deadly seriousness. New knowledge is always suspect.

We were astounded, confused, frightened, and even more indignant when people began to talk long distances over the air without even a wire! Meetings were held about the "ungodly wireless, a machine of the devil." We were still shocked—yet we had matured enough to be more receptive—when someone managed to send a quavery, wiggly black-and-white picture of events over the airwaves. When those pictures achieved perfection in sharpness and color, the fearful folk threw up their hands in resignation. "There is no end of it!" some of us cried. "What is this world coming to? Things are not the same anymore."

WHAT IS THIS WORLD COMING TO?

It is coming to even greater things, that's what.

Greater change. Based on inconceivably greater knowledge.

The moon walk was one proof; a planetary stroll may be next. Humanity's "conquering" the moon upset our romantic aeons-old superstition about that lovely satellite. "To you I'll croon, beside the lagoon, in June, under the moon." I even sang that myself! To Adele, down yonder in Houston, Texas, in college courtship. And we both lived to see some scientific killjoy walk on our moon and report back—by wireless—that it was nothing but airless dust and rocks. Not only was there no "man in the moon," it wasn't even made of green cheese. Disillusioning.

Very well. We all have to face up to realities. And the degree to which we oldsters do face up will· be the degree to which we have happiness and peace of mind in our twilight years. Truly trustworthy authorities today tell us that during the 19th century—which had its own marked acceleration in new knowledge—the sum total of human knowledge (all subjects) was doubling about once in 100 years. But soon after 1900 the rate accelerated so fast that by 1960 it was doubling every *five* years!

At about that moment, the emotional explosion truly began. By 1970 our minds were in a veritable whirl; not just the minds of us oldsters, but of youth as well. Newness had literally engulfed humankind. Positively, now, things were not the same anymore.

⟦ THE FAMOUS LINDAMAN GRAPH ON NEW KNOWLEDGE ⟧

Probably the best way to *try* to understand that acceleration in new knowledge is to consider the famous Lindaman graph. Edward Lindaman is a renowned space scientist, currently also a university president. He explains the graph thus:

Envision a graph of three perpendicular lines, drawn in proper proportion. Let the first line be just three inches tall.

Now let that three-inch line represent everything that human beings learned about everything, all subjects, the sum total of all human knowledge, from the day of Adam and Eve until the age of steam, which began around the year 1800 A.D. A line three inches high, representing millions of years of learning.

Then draw a second line representing the *additional* knowledge acquired by humankind from the start of the steam age to the start of the atomic age, about 1940. To be in proportion, this line must be about fifteen inches tall. Human beings had learned five times as much in 140 years as they had learned in all the millions of years before.

But now consider Dr. Lindaman's third line on the graph. Representing the still additional knowledge acquired in the barely three decades from the start of the atomic age (1940) to the year 1969—when he first made his graph—*the third line would have to be taller than the Washington Monument!*

The mind reels. It cannot envision such an astronomical concept, such an overwhelming new increase in human knowledge.

Certainly the minds of us folk who can remember horses and buggies, and bustles and milk churns and kerosene lamps, are thrown into a dither by such a consideration. But so, indeed, are the minds of our middle-aged children, and of people under the age of forty and on down through the teens. New knowledge —the vastness of it! Comparable only to the concept of the uncountable stars and their quintillions of light years distance from us; or to the immeasurable grains of sand beside the seas. Our feeble brains tend to stall. Confused, alarmed by it all, millions of us have turned our backs on knowledge, seeking comfort in a flight from change.

⟦So What's New?⟧

It is fascinating now to consider some of the *specific* changes that are developing right under our noses, though not yet generally recognized.

For example, the telephone as we know it, wonderful though it is, is obsolete. The poor thing is largely tied down by wires still.

But the telephone of the 1990s very probably will be about the size of a pack of cigarettes and will be worn on your wrist.

When you wish to speak with a friend in, let us say, Rio de Janeiro or Calcutta, you will touch a series of small buttons. Instantaneously a signal will leap from you to Telstar to Telstar, thence to the telephone on your friend's wrist. His photo will appear on your two-inch screen—in full color and three dimensions, sharp and clear—and yours on his screen. "Hi there!" you will say cordially. "How are things in your part of the earth this morning? It is bright and sunny here." As casually as that! Do you consider that a preposterous bit of science dreaming? Beware! Because it is virtually perfected already.

Or the postal service—that too is now obsolete. Indeed it is so inefficient as to be comical as well as costly, taking a ridiculous two days to get a letter across town, and two to ten days to get it delivered across the country even with airplanes.

But it has already been tested and proven easy to write a letter in New York and have it delivered in Los Angeles in thirty minutes! Facsimile reproduction, of words and colored pictures, instantaneously, received anywhere on earth, rolled into a tube and shot out to the home or office across the continent, all in ten to thirty minutes.

Or the newspapers—those bulky, laborious, costly things now dropped at our door (if the boy misses the roof!) are doomed to disappear soon, praise God. Instead, the "paper" will roll out of a smallish machine in our living rooms, sharp and clear in color, a new one every hour if we wish.

Television. Very soon—no bulky, dangerous, costly box. Instead, a flat screen, four to six feet wide, against any wall, portable, full color, and 3-D, with a recording device so that you can repeat any show later if you wish.

THE DELPHI METHOD: REASON, IMAGINATION, FAITH

As of this writing, the General Electric Company has 200 physical scientists, economists, and sociologists hard at work, spending nearly $10,000,000 a year, to determine what is most likely to happen by the year 2000. The Rand Corporation, cooperating with the United States Air Force, is spending nearly double that amount in the same study. An immense computer program to determine details of life in A.D. 2000 is under way at the University of Illinois.

Those agencies, and others, are getting their answers from the past and the present, by what is called extrapolation. They use the "Delphi Method," meaning a consensus of the forecasts by many thousands of the world's smartest scientists. They draw on reason, on imagination, and on faith.

So what news have they for us?

Typically—in the year 2000 wheels and highways will largely have disappeared. Envision a nation without automobiles, less than thirty years from now! If you

33

can; I can't, but as we kids used to say in my East Texas small-town homeland, "I ain't right bright." Those scientists *are* right bright.

The wheel has been civilization's symbol for many thousands of years. But in a couple decades, the prediction is, we will all be going from place to place by hovercraft—smallish airborne "cars" comparable only to the present storybook things we call flying saucers. Don't ask me how they will operate! As I confessed just above, I don't know nothin', I just work here, reporting what the brainy ones do know.

And what about freight trains, buses, high speed trains, jet airplanes? They will be gone, as obsolete as the horse and buggy is now. Ballistic transportation will be "delivering" anywhere on earth within forty to sixty minutes, we are told. All right, I won't argue it, and neither must you. If in 1910 you had told me there could ever be such a thing as perfected color television—whoo!

How Is Your Health Here Lately?

Virus diseases, bacterial diseases, will be eliminated by the year 2000—praise the Lord again.

Even if you and I aren't here to enjoy the promised freedom from head colds, our heirs will be. If a grandson or granddaughter a generation from now needs a new heart, kidney, knee, hip, backbone, stomach, brain —yes, even brain—drop down to the parts bank and have a replacement! No problem; just routine then. Oh of course I am oversimplifying, for emphasis. But most of those miracles are already coming to pass, and the

34

scientific know-how is expanding and improving almost hourly right now.

You who are reading this probably are an old man or an old woman. Chances are you were born back close to the time of the First World War. If so, then you now probably have assorted aches and pains, due to what we used to call rheumatism but now call arthritis, or to some similar ailment. You may have asthma, or diabetes, or pernicious anemia, or heaven knows what. Well, bless you, take comfort in the virtually certain fact that your now small grandchildren will be free of all those problems. "Malpractice" suits to the contrary notwithstanding, our doctors are keeping in the forefront of progress. As you well know, many old-time diseases already have been practically eliminated. And what of eyes, ears, teeth? Dearly beloveds, I have a beautiful granddaughter in college who has perfect vision. But at age two an eye infection would surely have blinded her in one eye—if. If our ophthalmologist hadn't removed the cornea from a seventy-two-year-old man who had just died, carried it into our grandbaby's operating room, and hemstitched it onto her eyeball! Incredible! The age of miracles? It is only beginning.

Now what of such evils as air pollution and smog? In the year 2000 about twelve great power stations will be generating all the energy used in the entire country, and the heat from them can lift air inversions so high that all pollution will be gone. Moreover, those stations can so effectively control weather that rainfall can be had exactly when and where we want it in any quantity desired. The vast deserts around Las Vegas, Phoenix, El Paso, and even Death Valley will indeed be "blooming as the rose." You don't believe it? To tell you the truth, I don't either; I'm as old-fogeyish and hidebound as you are. But I didn't believe anybody would ever go to the moon, either.

HOLD ON TIGHT NOW AS WE CONSIDER "TIME RESTORATION"

One absolutely intriguing promise, not really new but rapidly being tightened down, is the concept of time restoration.

"What's that?" you ask. Well, hold on tight.

We know that all actions, all speech and other sounds, send out "waves" on varying frequencies. Such waves went out at electronic speed when Jesus was delivering his Sermon on the Mount.

Where are those waves now?

Scientists have proved that such waves do not just evaporate into nothingness. They exist forever. Moreover, they strike walls or cliffs or planets, and bounce back. All we have to do is devise a gadget that catches the bounce—and that is relatively easy. Soon, therefore —maybe in the lifetime of our own grandchildren—man will be able to tune to the proper frequency and hear that sermon from Jesus' own voice. Similarly, we shall be with the Pilgrims landing at Plymouth Rock; with Washington praying at Valley Forge; and with Lincoln remembering at Gettysburg.

No, don't look askance at *me*, do not glare or act appalled, do not frown in bewilderment or terror, do not scoff or say "impossible." Think. Would Julius Caesar have believed the promise even of a rifle, much less of an atom bomb? Wouldn't Henry VIII probably have beheaded you as a witch, if you had told his court that the world would someday have an automobile and a telephone? You and I likely will not live to enjoy time restoration, but our little grandpeople most likely will.

WHAT ABOUT THE COST OF ALL THOSE WONDERS?

Many elderly folk have become concerned, even indignant, about the vast sums of money spent on space exploration in recent years. Those folk are saying that the money could well have been spent on ending poverty and enriching life on earth.

Such a mistaken view can only lead to feelings of bitterness or depression.

Wholly new knowledge acquired as an unexpected "spin-off" of the space effort already is enriching our lives beyond anybody's fondest dreams. Here are just a few of many examples:

1. The endless portable or battery-operated devices in the typical home are being revolutionized. New battery technology, developed by space experts, now is providing instant, sure starts for such things as lawn mowers, chain saws, outboard motors, toys, and power tools. It has completely changed the recharging of batteries, or made recharging unnecessary. (I have a new car with a department-store battery that will never require additional water, and that carries a life-of-the-car guarantee.) Surprisingly, that same battery know-

how is even making exciting improvement in photographic processes.

2. Several astonishing new fabrics have been developed. One of them, just half a thousandth of an inch thick, can be folded into a packet the size of a pack of cigarettes for carrying in pocket or purse. Then it can be unfolded to cover a king-sized bed. Yet it is strong enough to be used for a stretcher, a window covering, or a tent. It is windproof, waterproof, excellent insulation against heat or cold, and costs very little.

3. Fires that burn clothing, kill people, and destroy homes and other structures, will soon be only a sad memory.

New fabrics, and especially new paints developed by the space wizards, will have made everything literally fireproof. One paper-thin fabric, worn on your torso, is so heat-resistant that if a blowtorch is turned onto it you feel nothing and no damage results. This alone justifies all the cost of the space effort.

In the same area, a new insulation for metal has been developed. It is so effective that if you pour steaming coffee into a pot covered with it and seal the opening, the coffee will have lost less than one degree of temperature in a *year*! That also staggers the imagination; yet it is a fact of our time.

To be sure, all of us cannot instantly have all these wonders for our home use. Factories must be built, supplies located, distribution made certain. But they are coming!

4. Cooking today is done inefficiently, from the outside in. Often the outside of a costly roast is burned

in order to make the center portion edible. Soon, though, all cooking will be from the inside out. A pin will be inserted into your roast for quick cooking outward.

And the same type of pin can be inserted for quick-freezing of any food. Marvelous, isn't it?

5. Longitudinal grooves in cement, developed for special need in earth landings of aircraft, already are being used on certain automobile speedways. In one test on a California freeway those grooves reduced wet-pavement accidents by 75 percent and fatalities by 97 percent. When you consider that traffic accidents have been costing more lives than wars, think what those grooves can mean!

The list could extend into the dozens, most of them of a type to evoke head-shaking incredulity. Yet they are not mere "science fiction" daydreams, they are here *now*, proven and being put to use. All we need is mass production and distribution.

That increase in human knowledge, that newness which is such an explosive emotional force on us, has by no means been limited to the field of science. Our world of today is not *just* a world of gadgets and mechanical contrivances. We also know far more about the mind and spirit of human beings than we ever knew before. The whole pattern of psychiatry and clinical psychology has been revolutionized since about 1950. Family-life guidance has taken on new dimensions. Religion itself is changed, not in basic verities, but markedly in the organization and dissemination of truth.

⟦THE HAVES AND THE HAVE-NOTS⟧

One result of all this vast new knowledge, say the authorities, is the social revolution that has engulfed the world during the past couple decades. Almost overnight the have-nots of the earth arose to demand equality with the haves. This has happened on every continent, at home and abroad. Through the new media of communication, the downtrodden were suddenly able to become informed and knowledgeable, so they arose to demand the betterment of their condition.

Many simply began to *take* from the haves. Others initiated marches and parades and political actions. Everywhere, the cry was—and still is—for a new day, a better life. And I am not arguing for or against its merit, I am just reporting to you that the uprising is here.

So much newness in every field, so much technological and sociological change, has confused and distressed millions of us who can remember the placid days before World War I, and even those before 1950. We simply didn't understand! And many of us still don't. The world has run off from us; things are not the same anymore.

⟦THERE ARE "SMALL" CHANGES TOO⟧

Finally, it is a further fact that many thousands of us old folk are disturbed by little changes right inside our own homes and families.

This facet of change is *not* new; our grandparents faced it, as did their grandparents. But it is still something of a traumatic experience when it comes *your* turn to leave the "old homestead" and settle into a retirement center, or perhaps into cramped quarters with your adult children. Grandmother may become tearfully attached to the symbols of younger years—"I cannot part with this old rocker; I used to rock my babies to sleep in it!" Or her wrinkled husband will want to move a ragged old sofa with him into his last home because for thirty years he has taken a nap on it on the back porch.

Such symbols become very real to us. They are not to be laughed at—and shame on you young spriggenses if you do laugh! For you too will face old age, sooner than you think. Change of location for home, change of daily routine, change of furniture, clothes, tools, cars, eating habits, and recreation, all these are potent factors for men and women who have become somewhat "sot in their ways." We cannot afford to become sot!

COMFORT IN THE MIDST OF CHANGE

How, therefore, can we comfort one another? We who are old do tend to cling together. Naturally we do. We gather in little groups and talk. We point to all the excitement around us, then shake our heads in wonder, and not a little anxiety. What's to be done?

A poll of the wisest among us shows that there is only one worthy answer: *we must cling to our faith, and we must maintain a sense of humor*. The matter of staying good-humored is extremely important to all of us, but right here and now let's inspect our faith.

"Faith" has several facets.

41

Foremost of course is faith in God. If you lack that, you had better restore it promptly, or you will never find peace. Go at once to your minister, priest, or rabbi, any reputable pastor of your choosing. Go also to the Bible, and rediscover the great promises, the magnificent assurances that are recorded there.

But you must also maintain a strong, secure faith in yourself! This is imperative. Without it, you will degenerate into a quavery old wretch whom nobody can love without abject pity, you will be only "half a personality," and you will surely have a miserable old age. So tell yourself that you like yourself, and that you will quietly and positively adjust to old age with dignity and self-respect.

For some of us, that won't be easy. Thousands of old folk tend to become leaners, loafers, freeloaders, even bums. They scowl a lot. They insist that their children or their government or *somebody* must support them financially and emotionally, whereas nobody, period, has any such obligation, so long as you are in good physical and mental health. Nor can you "pose." You cannot delude yourself, or others, by turning into a hypochondriac. Not if you wish to maintain faith in yourself, not if you hope to maintain self-respect, not if you yearn to be happy in your remaining years.

Finally, you must indeed have faith in other people.

What other people? Your relatives, of course. Your friends. Your acquaintances. Your village or town or city, your county, state, nation, world. In short—*you must have an abiding faith in humanity.*

Maintaining that will keep you from degenerating into a sour old personality, an unlovable pessimist.

Tell yourself this: "Well, even if I don't understand all this newness around me, all this change in human society, I am glad to be living in the most *interesting* period of human history. I can hardly wait to see what's going to happen next. And I want to be a part of it."

No, "things are not the same anymore." And come to think of it—isn't that a wonderful fact for our old-age enrichment!

4.

It's a Big Matter
of Money

You bet it is, Buster. Or Betty. Or whatever your name is, and whatever your age is, and wherever you live. Money!

And don't give me any philosophical gobbledygook, saying there are many things more precious than money. There are, of course. Such as love. And for sure—faith. And dew-kissed roses, and a glowing sunrise, and the song of the meadowlarks.

Nevertheless, you just try buying groceries or paying the rent with any of those! You must indeed appreciate the beauties of life, for they will nourish your psyche, within the letter of the law make easy prey of her.

〚 STARTING WHEN? 〛

Financial preparation for old age should, of course, begin when we are about twenty-one.

But at the age of twenty-one, none of us is ever going to get old. By some blessed miracle, the matter simply does not enter our minds or our conversation; or if it does, we deal with it only in a joking manner. The world is so much upon us, so demanding of all that we can earn, that we give virtually no thought to tomorrow, much less to forty years hence.

By the age of thirty, we usually achieve a somewhat

44

more solid maturity of mind and do begin to admit that old age cometh. The big breakpoint, however, is forty. Overnight, it seems then, we are *old*. In our own estimation we have left youth behind, we are at the top of the hill and henceforth we can only accelerate downward. And lo, we have made no provision for senility and helplessness. Even now, we can't "save" much, if anything. Both Junior and Sister are ready for college, and tuition has skyrocketed. Moreover, your mate's mother is widowed and must move in with you, or perhaps be put into a retirement home—at your expense, because her husband left her very little. Nevertheless, you the forty-year-old couple do impulsively buy some kind of old-age insurance (not nearly enough, as it turns out) and start assiduously to save up for your senior years. Such is the standard pattern.

To our credit, we are fairly consistent in this belated savings effort. We are mildly frightened, so we do indeed try to put a little aside. Savings accounts today are at an all-time high. Social Security has literally forced us to save for old age—the money is first extracted from your pockets and then given back to you later—but we also realize that it isn't likely to be enough.

Therefore, in our earning forties we often buy a piece of land, hoping its value will inflate. Or we make regular deposits in some savings and loan association, or one way or another bury little sums under a figurative fence post. The upshot is, not nearly as many people are dependent in old age today as fifty or so years ago, in terms of population percentage. We are a thriftier people, in spite of our often wild and foolish spending.

Even so, many modern seniors find that their preparations are inadequate. In the 1930s the alluring magazine advertisements urged us to "Buy this insurance so that you can retire on $250 a month and live a life of luxury." Oh boy! *At that moment in time* (as the Watergate rascals so often intoned while hedging) $250 a month was like a fortune. But at *this* moment in time, as a result of continuing inflation, it buys a lot less. The dollar of 1940 became thirty-seven cents. The $800 luxury sedan of 1940 (I paid $830 that year for a De Soto) became the $4,800 sedan of 1970 and the $5,600 sedan of 1975. And the Cadillac? It leaped from a massive $3,000 to—heaven help us—a colossal not-worth-it $12,000, and is still climbing. All other commodities leaped in proportion—food included, need I remind you.

This has caused a profound shock wave through the ranks of the elderly, an anxiety, a worry, a fear that is entirely justified. Ask any banker, or any retirement-center manager. Old couples by the thousands keep streaming in, seeking advice about how to handle their lifetime savings which, though once quite promising, now seem woefully small.

⟦THE DANGEROUS "CON" MAN⟧

Seeing opportunity in that situation, dishonest "con" men and women have swarmed onto the old folk with gyp investment schemes. "We can double your money in six months," they promise glibly. "You will have a guaranteed mortgage, you can't lose." Or "Put your money into this new land development and you will not only earn 15 to 20 percent interest, you will have a home free."

How alluring! And how ridiculous. Widows especially are tempted by such fancy promises—the salesperson is so nice, so sweetly sympathetic and helpful, "just like one of my own children." But this kind of widow—extremely common—had little or nothing to do with managing the family finances before her husband died. Now, in a deep emotional state, she cannot think with caution. Thus the gyp "investments" that stay just within the letter of the law make easy prey of her.

The only comforting counsel I can give you is— beware.

Never act hastily. *Do not sign any paper whatsoever* until you have had expert guidance from a reputable individual or firm. Who is reputable? Not the stranger brought in by the salesperson! Never the well-dressed, smooth-talking man or woman who offers fancy "credentials."

Refuse to sign. Take time; take a week at least, no matter what rush the salesperson tries to put on you. Go directly to the nearest bank; ask for the manager and tell him your money problems, tell him about that sales approach from person or persons unknown to you. Or hire a reputable attorney to investigate for you.

When you sit with that banker, ask what rate of interest the bank is paying on savings deposits. Go also to the nearest savings and loan association and do the same; these often pay a slightly higher rate. (You can safely make this inquiry by telephone too.) If you deposit money in either, be sure that such deposits are guaranteed by the Federal Deposit Insurance Corporation for banks, or its equal for savings and loan firms. This is vital to your financial security. Do not let some uninsured firm tempt you with glib assurances that it has an even safer investment opportunity for you. Beware the con man!

〖 Ah Yes, the Stock Market! 〗

If you have only a few hundred or a few thousand dollars, you very likely will be tempted to "play the stock market" because a promise of fast profits is held out. If this happens to you, stall. Put off the salesperson again. Take a few days to consider. After all, what do you know about stocks and bonds?

Truth is, nobody knows anything about them, for sure. Even the so-called blue chip stuff is dangerous. Buying those "safe" papers can bust you quicker than a slot machine in Las Vegas; and with less fun for you! Oh you *might* make money; you often hear of people who do. But you? Can you, madam or sir in old age, afford to gamble?

Don't try stocks and bonds unless you can afford to lose without being financially hurt. That is a positive, hard-boiled rule of common sense. Any stock market is a gambling place. You can never learn to "beat it"—certainly not by listening to a glib salesperson, however honest he may be, or by "just dropping in" at the office and reading today's reports. Repeat: Gamble only if you can afford to lose, whether it be stocks and bonds or dice or poker or bridge or any other stupidity.

〖 Managing Your Properties 〗

Many retirees have been blessed with valuable prop-

48

erties, such as houses, vacant lots, farm lands, rental buildings. These are assets. They can indeed carry you through old age.

But if you are a widow, or a man who has not been accustomed to managing properties, then by all means hire a trained person or licensed property firm and pay the required fee. Ask your attorney about such firms or individuals.

Again, you can seldom be guided by some loving family member or friend, because he or she likely is unacquainted with the market situation and with your needs. Once more, take time. Check out the situation thoroughly. Mismanagement can bankrupt you quicker than the roulette wheel can.

Not even your beloved pastor can help you in most property management needs, because he himself is notoriously limited here. But he might know a reputable banker or other person at home in the financial world. If he recommends one, make a separate, second check on the one recommended, just to be sure.

Wise investments and sound handling money or property always require the most cautious, careful consideration. And I assure you, old friend, that you would be appalled to know how many of us elders make fools of ourselves here.

〚Day-to-Day Spending〛

Similarly, intelligent day-to-day spending—just the routine of buying groceries and clothes and medicines —demands care, if your money reserve is not abundant.

"Impulse buying" is the great temptation here. (This is also true for newlyweds; ask any banker.) That means, we buy on impulse, without thinking, without considering actual need or desire. Something is flashy, is packaged most alluringly. It is advertised as virtually indispensable for our health or safety or happiness or general welfare. Or, it is simply eye-appealing; it is something we have not had heretofore, and we haven't many more years to live, so why not just buy it and enjoy it while we still have time.

Okay. If you can truly afford it. But you can also end up in the poor house (whatever that is nowadays!) if you throw money around carelessly. Happily, most old folk do not really need much, compared to young marrieds who are in the business and social stream. Consider "things." Do you really need a fancy $9000 limousine, or could you forget about status and be happy with a compact costing one-third as much? At your age you are not likely to be doing a lot of hard traveling by automobile, so why do you want a gas-guzzling freight car just to impress yourselves and a few neighbors? Why do you want a costly sterling silver tea set, when you still cherish your fine china that has been loved all these years? Why must you have a custom-made gown or suit from a prominent tailor, instead of an appealing one "off the rack"? Is showing off—vanity—so important to you? Will such spending really bring you any genuine happiness or peace of mind in your senior years? In some such quiet manner, we must continually challenge ourselves.

Excellent clothes, becoming costumes for both women and men, can be chosen with good taste and minimum money wastage. This does not demand frumpishness or a poverty look. It does require some quiet, careful, diligent shopping. Which, heaven knows, can be fun for any woman, and almost any graying old gentleman.

⟦ YOUR SWEET LITTLE HOUSE ⟧ BY THE SIDE OF THE ROAD

Let's see, now, how does that go? "We'll build a sweet little nest, somewhere in the West, and let the rest of the world go by." That's it! How we used to croon, in June, under the moon. Remember?

But now, dear God, how those "sweet little nests" have skyrocketed in cost! For both sales and rentals.

Your housing in old-age years is so closely tied in with money and inflation, and is so important to you, that we must discuss it in detail in the next chapter. I have talked with hundreds, thousands, of aging folk nearing retirement. Far more than half of them have said, "We will always eat. But I'm not sure where we can afford to sleep."

5.

Where You Must Live

Choosing a residence for their last years on earth can be the most unsettling and disturbing experience that an old couple must face. "We will always eat, but where will we sleep?" Where, indeed! And at what cost in output of money and energy? By whom?

The matter seldom comes up before we are fifty. We *have* a house, however humble, however grand. In it we feel comfortable and secure. If somebody mentions the future, we tend to smile and speak from the top of our minds—"One thing is sure. We will move to a warmer climate." For nine-tenths of us that lurks inside us as a kind of latent dream.

There's even a joke about it. It seems that, in northern Wisconsin one winter day, an old couple was sitting in their chilly living room looking out at the ice-covered trees and the deep snow. Papa was worried. "Honey," he said, tremolo-voiced, wallowing in sentiment, "if one of us should die, what would the other'n do?" The old gal answered him with asperity—"I don't know what you'd do, Henry. But if you die, I'm gonna move to sunny California."

It is not merely funny, either. Millions have felt precisely as that old lady did, and have acted accordingly;

they have moved to California. Or to Arizona or Florida or some other area with year-round warmth. We can't blame them.

Millions of others have refused to face the matter so realistically. Papa has merely grinned, shrugged, and said that when he retired "We'll build a sweet little nest, somewhere out in the West." A vague promise; a sop to his conscience for procrastination.

All right. I loved that song. Still do. Still whistle it when I walk the nearby golf course "roamin' in the gloamin'" with my Adele at end of day. Still sing it lustily when we men of the Kiwanis Club wallow in nostalgia. I am probably the most sentimental slob you could ever meet; I can get tearful just humming "Always." Frankly, I hope you are like that too. Sentiment. Never belittle it. Never cease to cherish it, in yourself and in your aging mate.

But doggone it, old friends, your old-age *housing* must be given careful, realistic study, just as your buying of other things. If you are not truly rich, you can be truly gypped. You can sign papers that will become a heavy burden on your shoulders until you die.

Ask yourselves this: Won't a cute, smallish cottage or apartment do as well for you, or even better, than an elaborate mansion in Status Manor? The latter might have twice as much room—maybe six bedrooms and a drawing room and a big dining room and a terrace and all that. But who is to clean it, "housekeep" it? Mother —Grandmother—is aging. *She* shouldn't have that responsibility. So hire help? What help? Nowadays, domestic servants are not merely an endangered species, they are virtually extinct! And what about mainte-

53

nance—you know, the electrical repair, the recurrent plumbing problems, the leaky roof (even new roofs can leak), the cracked driveway, the peeled-off paint, the planting and cultivating of flowers, the endless mowing and trimming of shrubbery, trees, and grass? Is Father —Grandfather—up to all that? Or can he afford to pay for it, even if workmen can be found?

Adele and I might well have afforded a big home. We *had* a big home. Five bedrooms, four baths, huge lot; a picturesque Indian-style adobe—wonderful for family living when we had three ebullient daughters and were ourselves still young. But in retirement, we opted for a lovely small apartment, with exterior maintenance all done by the retirement-center corporation (for a small fee that I pay). She and I together do what little housekeeping is needed; takes us only two or three hours a week. We love it! We feel safe, with many near neighbors. A sweet little nest, somewhere in the West—literally. Happily.

Yours can be somewhere in the East. Maine, say. Or Virginia. Or Florida. Or forsooth, in Alaska or Hawaii or Wisconsin, or Quebec or British Columbia or Saskatchewan. It isn't where that matters, it's what. So choose a last "home place" where you can live in dignity without pretense. And make yourselves be happy there.

That, of course, is easier said than done, because many psychological factors enter into the matter. On top of everything there is the sudden new thrust of loneliness. Too many of our friends have died off. Our children now live 1,200 miles away. Even the beloved pastor who counseled us for years has moved to another parish. And here we are, stuck in this old barn of a house with three or four or more bedrooms and we rattle around in it, lost. We don't even know the next-door neighbors anymore—probably they are nice enough, but much too young and too busy to bother with us.

Thus the lamentations, the growing anxieties, the fears. I must have heard them from eight out of every ten couples I have interviewed.

They definitely get worse when one mate dies. The one left alone in the old family house (of whatever size and location) is truly forlorn.

⟦ So What's to Be Done? ⟧

Your first step is to admit that the problem exists. Recognizing any dragon is the first move toward slaying him.

Admit that you *are* getting along, you *are* likely to be unhappy trying to maintain the old place, rather piteously hoping to reverse the march of time or maintain the status quo.

So—calmly tell yourselves that, yes, this house, this apartment has now served its purpose in our lives. It has been a good place. We have loved it, we have reared our children here, we have had a "heap o' livin'" in it that made it truly a home, Mr. Guest. But it is now time to close out that chapter in our book of life, and start a new one. The new one can be much simpler and more fitted to old-age needs.

With that sensible attitude, you have no critical problem at all. You have a powerfully motivating eagerness—for a new life, in perhaps a new and happier-than-ever environment.

⟦ Shall You "Live with the Children"? ⟧

For many of us, Junior and Sister have been wonderful. You taught your children about selfless love and sharing, about gratitude, about faith and reaching for excellence. Now they themselves are prosperous adults with their own fine families, and it would be a pleasure for you to have a closeness with them during your final years. Moreover, they have said that you could move in. A room will be prepared for Mom and Dad. You would have your own private bath, your own TV set, maybe even a little kitchenette. You would be part of the modern young family.

But beloved old friends—you wouldn't like it.

You might think you would, in anticipation, and even in first experience. But I guarantee you, such togetherness would quickly pall. On both you and the young folk. In theory—no; in actuality—yes. The exceptions are very few.

Psychologically, *it is impossible for two families to occupy the same home in harmony*, no matter how much all of you love one another, no matter how close you have always been. Sentiment can rarely control the matter. You have heard of the generation gap? It is as old as the race. Adam and Eve surely felt the distance between them and their recalcitrant sons—"What hast thou done to thy brother?" father Adam had to de-

56

mand of his son Cain in shock and horror. No, you will not likely face murder. But there will almost certainly develop a coolness, a standoff kind of politeness at best, between the two sets of adults. Mainly because you simply can't let each other alone. Even if you oldsters try hard and force yourselves to stay out of the children's lives, you are neveretheless always *there*. A careless look, a mere facial expression, can imply criticism —unconsciously—on either side. Soon you will sense that you are a perhaps silent but very real and costly responsibility, an unintentional burden. Resentment is almost inevitable. Actual experience has provided abundant tragic proof.

⟦Where, Then?⟧

A separate home or apartment not too far from the adult children is often satisfactory. Next door is still too close; even the next block is. Across town—so that you can see each other often yet not impinge on one another daily, not get in anybody's hair—is usually a happy arrangement. The closeness can still be felt, without risking the resentment that builds up when you are too much under foot.

Truth is, the generation gap is a God-given blessing in disguise. We don't *need* to, can't be expected to, live the lives of our children. Two generations never have seen and never will see eye-to-eye.

About the two families not living together—there are, of course, important exceptions. If you or your mate is crippled physically or mentally and close care is needed, if you are poverty-ridden or "poor" and simply cannot afford a separate place, then a last home with your children is indeed acceptable. If all the persons concerned are high in spiritual development, the mutual sacrifice can even become exalting. There is abundant precedent.

But in the above discourse I was speaking of the vast majority of instances, as borne out by careful research and statistical studies and by personal observation. Wherefore, if at all possible—stay apart.

The exact type of new, smaller home you choose must be determined by cost and taste. Some old couples are wealthy. These often make the mistake of building a costly mansion after they have turned sixty or sixty-five. From my own acquaintances I can name at least five such couples. In each case the results were disastrous; the old marriage simply fell apart. One was in that "high society" affluent-population town of Carefree, Arizona; the old gent spent more than half a million on a "castle" in the hills, and before it was finished his old wife had divorced him. An even more conspicuous example was in Phoenix. There, a nationally renowned financier, gray-haired and rather testy, spent well over two million on a showy dwelling atop a hill. Heavens, it even had a swimming pool inside the master bedroom! That poor soul never got to live there. *His* wife got fed up and left him, too. Anyway, whatever would they have done with twenty bedrooms and acres of space? In their sixties? Tragically, they were reaching—or he was. Not for excellence in living, but for escape, for prestige and respect which inherited money never brings. If you are wealthy, sir and madam, and you still "rattle around" in a costly old home where you cannot make servants stay—reorient your thinking. You have worshiped things that are physical rather than spiritual. You *think* the rest of us envy you. We don't. We pity you.

⟦ But You "Have Money"? ⟧

Even if you have it in unlimited quantities, a compact efficiency place is advised for your old-age years. This need not be prohibitive in cost. Transience, temporariness, being the order of the modern day, dwellings are being built for short-use expectancy. Ours is an especially mobile society. Today the average time for any house to be occupied by the same family is less than five years. Fifty years ago and before, a house was expected to "stay in the family" for three or four generations. The automobile and the airplane changed that, making us a go-go society. Hence if you do have money and do build yourselves a "nice" (meaning costly) new home, chances are you won't stay in it much. Studies show that you will be heading off on a Caribbean cruise, or for a long look at Japan and Hong Kong, or for basking on the Riviera beaches. Verily, restlessness is the hallmark of our old-age affluent set. The fine home you build often becomes something that pride has built, and does not really upgrade your life.

This is not to say that you well-to-do old folk must retreat into a monastic life of self-denial. It is simply a warning that an expensive new home in old age can become burdensome, because of maintenance and servant problems, if no other. Self-delusion is ever a danger in

59

building such a home for retirement years. So even if you do "have money," think twice before spending it on housing.

⟦ BACK TO THE HAUNTS OF OUR YOUTH ⟧

For millions of us, regardless of money, one common first tendency at retirement time is to sell our home and furnishings, then trek back 200 or 2,000 miles to the environs of our youth. We were born and reared—let us say—in Henderson, Texas. That's a sweet, small-ish county seat town nestled among the redbud and dogwood blossoms, and how well I remember the magnolia trees with their blossoms bigger than a man's hat, wafting their strong perfume all over the area. In spring crimson clover carpets the rolling hills, mocking-birds sing, and trout leap in the ponds, and people are so friendly when they gather in the courthouse square. Ah yes. We went to school there, courted during high school days, went on to college, came back, got married, and worked our way up the economic ladder, until we found ourselves living in one of those posh "corncob-skyscraper" apartments in congested Chicago.

But now Henry has retired, and Chicago is windy and cold, and we daydream of our youth. "Let's sell out, Henry, and move back to Henderson . . ." It is a typical idea, a recurrent yearning. Don't do it.

Almost invariably, it would be a mistake. Such old folk are motivated solely by memories, the good times of childhood in the old hometown recalled. Actually, the times back there probably were quite rugged, but *that* memory has faded—thank you, Lord. Today's old-sters think of their own parents, resting now in the pretty cemetery at some quiet Maple Grove Church. They speak of the old peach orchard, where we kids used to climb up high and pluck rich soft juicy sweet-as-honey Elbertas, and mess up our clothes with a stain that would never wash out—and how Mama would fuss! They talk of the pond with the flat-bottomed rowboat, from which our big brothers taught us to catch perch; and of the hayloft high in the barn, which became a fort or a castle or any kind of play-pretend hideaway we wished. Ah, yes, those were the days; so let's return there for our happy years of retirement.

Don't go.

When you get back there, it will be hard to find any-one you know; harder still to find anyone who knows you. The peach orchard is now the site of a new high school. The pond was drained and a modern electronics plant built on the site. The barn has given way to a new six-lane highway. *We can't go home*! We can't re-verse the calendar. Not ever. Rarely, rarely, can we find or recapture the magic of yesteryear, even for a fleet-ing moment. Happily, we don't need to. The *new* years are the most wonderful of all.

〚 Why Not Rent a Place? 〛

It is not imperative that you *own* any home; millions of homes are rented. Many elderly folk can qualify for rent subsidies in publicly-financed private housing projects. If you need this financial help, inquire around for names of rent-supplement housing sponsors (serv-ice clubs and churches). Investigate locations of proj-ects even if they are only on the drawing boards, be-cause there is often a waiting list.

Do not overlook public housing projects. In some instances rentals can be very low indeed. Do not be dismayed by the "poverty" stigma which you may think attaches to this type of housing. Remember, you have long paid taxes, against just such a need. Anyway true poverty is a matter of the spirit, not of money.

Decades ago the civilized world was blighted with what were called poor houses, meaning charity places. In jest—or half-jest only—we would tell one another that we were "going over the hill to the poor house" if times didn't get better. Well, times were what we made them, then as now. And quite a few thousand luckless folk did so go over that hill. Most poor houses were owned by the local government or by churches, and their inmates were objects of pity. The "accommodations" in them were such as to shame their communities. A few still exist.

But we have come a long way. Social Security and various food, housing, and aid programs have all but ended those horrors of a century ago. Our government has made itself into a kind of hydra-headed Robin Hood; it takes from the rich to help the poor. And we decent folk cannot find it in our hearts to condemn that kind of socialism. The only danger is that it be overdone. The government is trying hard to discourage freeloaders—among the administrators as well as the beneficiaries! Meanwhile if you, an impecunious retiree and mate, need such help, by all means apply for it. You are entitled to a clean, sanitary, dignified house in which to live—if circumstance has made you unable to provide one for yourselves.

These are fabulous!

I declare to you, aging friends, they really are. Retirement centers are a miracle of the second half of the twentieth century, a blessing for sure. They are mushrooming all over, especially in such sunny areas as southern California (remember where the old gal in Wisconsin said she was going when her Henry died?) and in even more sunny Arizona and Florida. Their names have in just a few years become a part of the language—Sun City (there are several of these), Rancho Bernardo, Quaker Gardens, White Sands, Casa Mañana, Senior Towers, La Verne Center.

If you and your mate can afford one of these—go! They are so far superior to any other arrangement that there is no comparison. Some retirement centers tend to gyp people by overcharging; so do investigate, do not buy impulsively. Many are moderate in cost. A few are only for very wealthy people.

It is preposterous to assume that such centers "are nothing but hotbeds of senility," as some stupid critic declared a few years ago. Honest sociologists did worry at first. They feared that any town inhabited solely by old people would indeed develop an atmosphere of gloom and doom and hopelessness. Such a town, the critics said, would be like a concentration camp, a place to coerce unwanted oldsters into sitting down and waiting for death.

As it turned out, quite the opposite is true.

This is because elderly people, far from being

gloomy, are in fact the *most* capable of enjoying life. As a class they are far less uptight and fearful than teenagers are, because they have learned to cope with life's vicissitudes. They are far more relaxed than the middle-aged parents, because they are not so laden with responsibilities, they have "been through the wringer" already; they can slow down, sit on the front porch of that apocryphal sweet little nest somewhere in the West, then *literally*—if they wish—let the rest of the world go by. They—we—are the only class of people who *can* do that!

Thus the retirement town where Adele and I live, far from being a hotbed of senility, is more nearly a hotbed of hilarity and activity. We have about 20,000 population—*all with a common cause*, the business of living our twilight years with dignity and good humor and grace. We all understand that, so we help one another. We are not harassed by minute-to-minute demands on our minds and muscles and nerves. We are, forsooth, retired! And we love every moment of it.

It is as instinctive for retirees to flock together as it is for blackbirds, cattle, kindergarten children, the high-school set, young matrons, attorneys, doctors, merchants, or any other group. Even the fish of a species swim in "schools." So there is nothing unique about us old folks' enjoying one another's company—and enjoy it we do! We probably have the wildest bridge games in America, right in our retirement towns. Not to mention a hundred other recreations, hobbies, and educational courses. Basically, it is these gregarious instincts that have made retirement centers such a standout success.

The sharp-minded economists who developed the centers are mostly quite young, under fifty. They "think modern." Meaning, they sensed that we old fogys did not want old fogy atmosphere in our towns, we wanted late-twentieth-century living. Thus it is that Adele and I constantly marvel at our good fortune, as do all our neighbors. We think we live in the world's most beautiful small town—and we have traveled widely, looking. Every home, every apartment building, every structure, is an architectural gem, restrained but elegant. There are no TV aerials, no signboards, no power poles (electricity comes underground). Elaborate gardens, with shrubbery and trees and vines and flowers beyond belief, are kept manicured to spit-and-polish perfection. We ourselves have the option of landscaping around our individual homes or of letting the corporation workmen do it. We also have virtually perfect police security; outlawry in our town of 20,000 is almost nonexistent, partly because each person who enters must be carefully identified, night and day.

These are just a few of the many advantages, and most of the retirement towns are like that, though each has an individuality of its own. Escape areas? These are in effect the grandest that have ever been conceived! No, they are not charity places, but most are moderate in cost. If you have even a few thousand dollars saved up or can raise a few on properties that you own or possibly as a gift from your prosperous children, you are in! Provided—provided—always provided—you have a reputation as a decent law-abiding citizen. Strict screening keeps out the undesirables. Regardless of your money, it takes about a month of quiet investigation before you can be admitted as a citizen of our retirement town. Economically, most of our citizens are low-income or middle-income; a few are wealthy. But spiritually and intellectually, our citizens are cream-of-the crop.

⟦ Start Your Own Center ⟧

To be sure, not every elderly couple can enter one of the posh centers described above. Nor do you need to feel slighted if you can't. If you are ruled out by preference or lack of money, for example—then do what also has been done successfully in many areas. Contact six, ten, twenty, any number of couples, and "flock together'" somewhere. Take over two floors of an apartment building. Or hire a contractor to make a little suburban center just for your small group, with private homes and a central swimming pool with recreation rooms. You don't have to move into an impressive retirement town; you can have an old folks' center on just one block. "Try it," as the feller says, "You'll like it." It is already a tried-and-tested thing.

Most such small centers do not have or need names. They are simply people of compatible personalities, ages and economic levels who establish homes near one another for mutual comfort. We need that comfort. Mary at the age of seventy-three needs the understanding friendship of Alma who is seventy-six, and both of them can help Louise adjust. Louise and Tom have just moved in, and she is barely sixty, and a trifle scared.

First thing you know those three have a round-robin series of dinner parties going, once a week in one couple's home. Then follows recipe swapping, and happy plannings for a picnic in the hills, or theater parties, or flower plantings. Thus the fellowship builds.

Meanwhile, what of their husbands? Unless they are congenital bums, the typical twenty-four-hour day is too short for them. "I resent the necessity for sleep," grinned old pal Luke Longwell two years ago. "Neighbor Jim Hale and I are adding a room to his house. When it's finished, we will add one to mine. His will be a lapidary laboratory for both families. Mine will be arranged for ceramics, including a kiln. The wives are pushing us to hurry."

That's the way it often works out: retirees, with mutual interests, doing what they have always yearned to do, and now have time for. It is a consideration that should be studied when you buy, build, or rent a house for your last years.

⟦ Bells of Reassurance ⟧

"But I am a widow," you may say. Or, "I am a widower."

It is a sad state, yes indeed, for any old person thus suddenly to be alone on earth. We can all envision the onslaught of loneliness. We also know that the first question usually asked of a mate after the funeral is, "What will you do, where will you live?"

The very best answer, long-range studies have proved, again is—do not move in with "the children" (that is, your adult children's home) if this can possibly be avoided. No matter how deep the love is, an old mother or an old father living with young folk can become a bone of contention, a restriction, a resented responsibility. There are millions of instances of proof. Visit the young folk for a month or two during the acute period of grief, if you wish. But unless your declining health or your destitute financial position demands it, move out soon and resume living—alone, but not in loneliness. There's a difference.

The cold truth is—there are several advantages to living alone. We need not go into them here, because they vary with each individual, and each one of us is likely to discover them in due time.

But there are some common drawbacks, too. One major consideration for those who would live alone in a house or apartment is the necessity for maintenance. People who are really old can no longer climb up to repair the roof. Many cannot stoop or squat to weed the flower beds. Many old hands cannot hold the screw driver—or indeed see the screw—that holds the door lock on tight. Thus some kind of provision must be made for the physical necessities. This includes cooking and even marketing for food.

But the major factor in lone living is—fear.

That is quite normal, natural. "What if I fall and cannot get to a telephone? What if I have a stroke or a heart attack? I could lie there helpless for weeks before anybody discovered me. Then most likely I would be dead."

Very true! It is indeed cause for worry and fear, a *major* cause. It could happen to any of us.

So then—*arrange for "bells of reassurance,"* a simple solution to this problem:

One loner makes a friendly agreement with another loner to *telephone at least once each day*, preferably near sundown, just to be sure that each is safe and happy, just to have a pre-bedtime friendly chat, with bits of humor, with some laughter, some planning for tomorrow, anything at all that keeps the heart light. Talk one minute, or one hour. *Visit* by telephone—and thereby be reassured.

Mary calls one week, Jane the next; Henry calls one week, John the next.

If preferred, a third party can be hired (and often is) to do all the calling for a safety check. Wheelchair people or other shut-ins are ideal for this. Pay them a modest fee each month; help them get several customers. When you do not call or do not answer on any given day, the other party starts an immediate investigation.

Such bells of reassurance are ringing daily all across the country. Thus many lives have been saved, many critical needs met, even many suicides prevented. In my own apartment building of twenty-four families, a widow telephoned me one day to say that she was going to kill herself that morning. I got right onto that. It happened three years ago, and she is still alive, and happy.

Undoubtedly this telephone arrangement is the happiest security measure that has ever been devised for loners, regardless of age. In planning your housing for old age, by all means include it.

Not all homes, of course, can have telephones, for

one reason or another. I think of Old Man Devore. If he had a more correct and formal name, none of us ever heard it. But no matter, he was a kindly, uneducated, gentle fellow, much loved by his neighbors—the nearest one of which was on the next mountain about a mile away as the crow flies. (The crow? He is supposed to fly in a straight line, but I never saw one do it!) A nature lover, a hermit, a philosopher, a loner in a nice cabin, he just didn't want to come down to live in town in the flats. So his friends worried about him.

"Tell you folks what I'll do," he grinned one day at church, during coffee hour. "I will erect a flagpole in front of my house. Every sunrise I will raise the stars and stripes. Now across the way to the next mountain slope, live you Morrises with several kids. One of you take your telescope just before sundown every day and look across the canyon. If my flag is not flying—come git me!"

A happy idea for all concerned. Some way, in your own housing as a loner, plan to erect a "flag" every day, telephonic or otherwise—a daily check. That way, if you need it, somebody can come "git" you!

⟦We Need More than a Roof⟧

Positively, old folk need more than a roof.

All parties concerned must understand this. It is not enough to "turn them out to pasture" as if they were old work horses, needing only a place to eat and sleep. An architectural cubicle or two is not enough; retirement must be regarded as something geared to the *totality* of human need. A mere house, with no other considerations, may well contain psychological misery that no amount of physical comfort can offset. Many rich people in mansions become pitifully neurotic and even commit suicide.

To salve their consciences but evade their responsibilities adult children often do "provide a home" of some kind for Mom and Pop—then largely ignore them. This can happen even in Jewish families, where the tradition of venerating the elders is admirably strong. Among all religions, all races, rejection of the elders in spirit if not in physical form is all too common in this enlightened era.

Knowing this psychological factor in advance does much to reduce the menace of it. If you as Grandmom and Grandpop have not developed ideal rapport with your children over the years, you cannot expect to do it suddenly in time of need.

Let us hope that you do have a closeness, a true unselfish and reciprocal love, so that you will not be shoved aside and then ignored. But you can never *demand* that. You cannot get it by pleading, either piteously or cantankerously. "Duty" cannot enter into the matter; desire has to be the key. If the desire is missing in your children, then you must build an old-age house or home of your own, without self-pity, without nagging, whining, or accusing. Do not be vague about this; be positive.

So, plan accordingly, early. "Command the morning," yes; but also command the final years. If at all possible build, buy, or rent a home-apart for your final years. (Repeat: There are some valid exceptions.) Then as the famous old Christmas carol tells us—"let nothing you dismay."

71

6.

How Is Your Health?

Don't tell me.

That's the basic trouble with you old men and women —if we ask you how you are feelin', you tell us. Whereas in point of fact, we are not all *that* interested. Oh, to be sure, we are sorry about your arthritis, your gasid indigestion, your "irregularity," your slipped disc, *et cetera ad lib de luxe ad nauseam*. And out of routine courtesy we will listen patiently.

But we won't invite you to dinner tomorrow night, won't ask you to play golf or bridge. That reaction on our part is just human nature; self-pitying sick people get negligible sympathy from anyone.

So if I ask you, don't tell me. I am merely being polite. But have I told you about *my* health problem? Heavens, it is fascinating! I have to have this hernia operation, see, and the doctor said——

⟦ So Go Ahead
Talk It Out ⟧

Let me reverse myself. Go ahead and tell me. I promise—I will listen attentively. I will be bored stiff, but I will cluck sympathetically and say nice words. So will 99 percent of all our colleagues-in-years.

That's because we *understand*. We have been there.

We *are* there, millions of us, right now. We wish to heaven there was some way to help you, besides just letting you talk it off your chest. Bless you, old friend.

Statistically, the matter of health ranks from fourth to first place among the day-in, day-out concerns of aging people, especially those around seventy years old. Surprisingly, those past eighty generally have achieved "acceptance," hence do not dither about health so much. "How is your health?" somebody asked an eighty-one-year-old former movie star. The actress's perfect answer showed that she was gratefully counting her blessings: "I'm perpendicular."

Common sense tells us that poor health can become the foremost worry for any of us at any hour. We see illnesses and injuries all around us. We visit old friends in infirmaries, hospitals, wheelchairs, home beds. We see them limping, or hobbling on crutches and canes. We hear of heart attacks and cancers and broken bones and all manner of distressing ills.

Almost certainly you yourself have some ailments right now. If you are not in any actual pain, you at least will admit to waning energies—and let no pseudo-virile old geezer flex his muscles, grin fatuously, plunge into the swimming pool, then come up and try to tell you "It's all in your mind." Invariably he has been "psyched"—as modern youth slang says—by himself or by someone else. Privately, his knees are likely to be as weak as yours and mine, or worse; his self-delusions merely make him appear momentarily enviable. You and I—and he too, for that matter—need to be completely realistic and sensible. Self-delusion itself can become a serious form of illness.

73

So then, again, face up.

What's wrong with you? Your answer of course will be unique; no two of us have precisely the same health problems. But whatever yours are, you will get no relief, no comfort at all, until you do something to correct them.

Because illnesses are highly individual as well as highly technical, no specific health-cure procedures can be prescribed here. But I do urge you to avoid, at all cost, any hypochondriacal self-pity, any play for sympathy by thinking and speaking too much of your health problems. In the opening paragraphs of this chapter, I was not joking; I was, in fact, all too accurate. Talking constantly about your ills—whether you are asked or not—will alienate your family, your friends, even your doctor. If you are truly sick and need help, ask for it, yes. But do not dwell on the matter. Do not make an unpopular pest of yourself by becoming a complainer. Face up to your need; take charge.

Based on extensive studies of health among old folk, the counteractions taken against diseases, and the results thereof, here are some important suggestions:

Get a complete physical checkup every year, every six months if you are past sixty-five, more often if your doctor advises it.

That counsel of course is old-hat; we have heard it for decades. Yet generally we have not heeded it, and we still don't. We just let the matter slide. "I'm not sick," we tell ourselves and others. "Why should I see a doctor?"

The obvious but ignored answer is, "So that you won't *get* sick."

An ounce of prevention. A tightening of the hub before the wheel flies off, wrecking the wheel and killing you. It is the height of conceit to feel that *you*, by some strange miracle, are immune to ailments of the flesh and need no preventive attention. Going to a reputable physician every six months or so does not tag you as a hypochondriac. It simply means that you are repairing the roof before the rain falls; you are taking sensible precautions, in time. Heart attacks, cancer, "plumbing troubles," arthritis, obesity, any of many ailments do beset us who are old. The regular checkup can prevent, postpone, or alleviate them, if not actually cure them later. This is possibly the most important health truth for you to remember.

〚 Beware of Quackery 〛

A copper belt, worn around your waist or wrist, positively will *not* prevent or cure any ailment whatsoever. Yet millions of us (of all adult ages) waste millions of dollars each year on such hardware because of false advertising and misleading promises. Don't you do it.

"An apple a day will keep the doctor away"? Most likely, for us old folk, it will tend to cause excessive intestinal gas, and even pains. Fresh apples and fresh head lettuce are two of the no-nos in diet for many thousands of elderly folk, unquestioned authorities have declared. Yet those two items are known as "health foods"—which they may well be, for the young.

A diet study, then, can be made for you by a competent internist, and probably end many of your routine intestinal problems. Just don't let some quack get at you. Don't take guidance from a too-talkative friend. Get a reputable physician.

Make sure he is reputable *as of now*. We seniors tend to stick with the old "docs." But the old family friend who delivered your babies and treated you yourself when you were twenty-four to fifty years of age, may be a semisenile incompetent today. Even if he is alert and going strong, his knowledge may be ten years behind the times. A typical example: For years prior to about 1974, heart-attack victims were told and told and told that they had to eliminate most foods that caused cholesterol, because cholesterol brought on the attacks. So, a national plague of strict no-cholesterol dieting swept the land. But by late 1975 new findings—definite new studies by responsible scientific research teams—proved that cholesterol had virtually no effect on the heart, if any at all; in other words, a direct denial of the prior "knowledge." That news caused a grand stir. Old-hat physicians, "sot in their ways," were indignant. And that too was normal. It has always taken five to ten years for many of the medical fraternity members to accept new knowledge. Even a truly good and conscientious doctor, who is along in years, can be opinionated, inflexible, autocratic.

That has nought to do with the fact that you love him as neighbor and friend. Those fine old physicians of a century ago who "bled" our forefathers in treating almost any ailment, and who encouraged "laudable pus" in wounds instead of sterilizing them, were loved as friends even when unknowingly doing far more harm than good. Medical knowledge today is possibly twenty times greater than it was ten years ago. Has your old friend kept the pace? It is unlikely.

So—go to his son, who is a modern specialist, or to another of the "now generation" physicians. Science may save your life where sentiment couldn't; loyalty is not antiseptic.

In the highly profitable field of treating the sick, the honest "old doc" is not to be classified as a quack. Quackery is always incompetence, but incompetence is not necessarily quackery. However, there are areas in which sheer, blatant dishonesty is victimizing the public, especially us older folk who are too trusting. Here are three common ones:

1. The "patent" medicines.

Their overall advertising thrust is almost unbelievable. Billions of dollars are spent to make us spend more billions on pills, capsules, ointments, and nostrums that are worthless, or even harmful to us.

True, a few do give us "fast, fast, fast relief"—for a short-short-short time; then we need more of the same, which enriches guess who, and victimizes guess who. Some of these brand-name medicines have become almost household venerable, so self-deluding and dependent are we. But on April 10, 1972—typically—the front pages of our newspapers told us that the government had accused the makers of Anacin, Arthritic Pain Formula, Bayer Aspirin, Bayer Children's Aspirin, Bufferin, Excedrin, Excedrin PM, Cope, Vanquish, and Midol of misleading advertising that made claims of questionable scientific validity. This news shocked millions of us who had tacitly come to assume that such concoctions were sacred!

For your own sake, don't, don't, don't gobble advertised junk merely because some paid actor or actress comes on your screen and says it vastly improved his or her energy, efficiency, sex life, amiability, digestion, and general joie de vivre. When such advertisements face us on TV or newspaper or magazine pages, old folk especially tend to fall for their promises. In our yearning to "feel good again," we are much too gullible and trusting.

If you think you need any dosage for any purpose whatsoever, *be guided by your doctor*. Or you can become a pitiable "pilloholic" before you know it.

2. *The advertising dentist.*

It is possible—just possible—that some of the dentists who advertise their services are honest. And even capable. But the dental associations, the high-level practitioners, frown on all advertising—which should be your cue to be wary.

Again, you will be familiar with the questionable type. There he is, on your TV screen, looking ruggedly handsome and dependable, mature and kindly, much like your oldest son perhaps. He gives you a sales pitch about coming to one of his three or fifteen clinics. Painless extractions. Dentures fitted the same day. Easy payments.

You may not need any extractions at all, and no dentures. Very often, old teeth can be recapped. The quack dentist tends to be a "butcher" because of the quick money involved. Wherefore, as in getting a general medical practitioner, or any specialist for your body—including for sure any who will perform any operation—be certain that your dentist is in good repute with your county medical association. Protect yourself as well as your pocketbook.

3. *The better-hearing "clinic."*

You also see their advertisements every day. These tell us —truthfully—that at the age of sixty-five or over, one out of every seven persons needs one and probably two hearing aids: So hurry in, you fine senior citizens, and let us fit your ears with tiny invisible earphones which will enable you to hear perfectly and live zestfully again.

Don't go!

Don't go near such an office or "clinic" *until you have had a thorough examination, including what is called an audiogram* (detailed technical analysis of your individual hearing problem) *done by a reputable otologist* (a physician who is an ear specialist). This is very important to you, not only in saving you money, but in protecting your hearing ability. Check out your otologist by telephoning your local medical association; do not rely on hearsay.

If you just go first to the advertising "clinic" you may pay fifty to $1,500 for gadgets that do your hearing little or no good and could do actual harm. Advances in hearing-aid science have been phenomenal in recent years, so very probably you can expect some genuine help. Just be wary of the smooth-talking quack. In many instances, a simple operation can restore perfect hearing, with no gadget needed at all.

Bear this further fact in mind—*no* hearing aid, however costly, will restore your lost hearing to its youthful perfection. The very best any aid can do is enable you to "get by," to communicate with greater ease than you could without it. I myself wear two costly hearing aids, because I now have 41 percent hearing loss due to nerve deafness. Those little devices hanging on my ears cost more than $400 each (less expensive ones may be of comparable help). Even so—everything I hear through them sounds "tinny," metallic, unreal. Music is virtually a lost delight for me, as is any drama on the stage, almost any lecturer including preachers, and the use of the telephone. On the other hand, I have a telephone amplifier which helps; and strangely, I hear birdsongs perfectly. And for hearing my loved ones and friends I do not have to carry around a horrid big black "powder horn" thing, and stick it in my ear, then mutter "Eh?" every time you speak to me! Our deaf parents had to do that—remember?

Actually, I have been looking for one of those old-timey hearing horns. I could have some fun with it, say, at social gatherings. (I have a streak of clown in me anyway—ask my wife, poor dear.) Which reminds me of a story:

〚 Those Unforgettable Chimes 〛

It seems that the great First Presbyterian Church had a beautiful high tower, and every hour on the hour chimes away up there proclaimed the time of day and threw in a few bars of sacred music just for love and goodwill. Everybody in town cherished that music from the sky.

So okay, one day old Uncle Abner Zilch was walking near the church, and a friend met him. Uncle Ab was dang nigh teetotally deaf—his own appraisal of himself—but even with no hearing aids, he "done right well" most of the time. Thus the friend paused, smiled, shook hands, and in normal tone—while the chimes were ringing—said to the old man, "Good morning, Abner. Aren't the chimes beautiful?"

Uncle Ab said "Eh?" (Of course. All us "deefies" say "Eh?")

The kindly friend then remembered to speak louder: "I say, good morning, sir. And aren't the chimes making lovely music?"

Uncle Ab stood silent, trying to decipher that, but couldn't. So he said, "You'll have to talk louder."

So the friend really spoke out: *"I say, aren't the chimes beautiful!"*

Again Uncle Ab paused, frowning, then shouted to his friend, "You'll have to speak up, Sonny. *I cain't hear a word you are sayin', for them damned church bells!"*

That absolutely true apocryphal story has a moral for you and me, assuming you are partially deaf also. The moral is—adapt. Adapt with a sense of humor wherever possible. Do not *fight* deafness; learn to live with it, without resentment. Courteously say to strangers, "I must explain that I am partially deaf, so forgive me if I come close and listen." That gets you by.

When people ask about my deafness I often have another explanation: "One day my wife Adele told me she was going downtown to buy herself a Persian cat.

81

But shucks, we *had* a cat and didn't need another. Well, she came home with a new *purse and hat*! So I went forthwith to an otologist."

There also are several other areas of health concern for us citizens who have turned fifty or more. Below, I have reported on what studies show to be the most common ones, though not necessarily in the order of their importance to you individually.

Close to the top in universal interest, however, is—

⟦EXERCISE⟧

"I get my exercise," some wisecracking old coot is alleged to have boasted, "by helping carry my hard-exercising friends to the graveyard."

Well, he has a point. But it is a minor one, of rather isolated application. It is possible to live a sedentary life—just settin' and doin' nothin,' not even thinkin', day in and year out—and live to be ninety years of age. But for each one of that type who reaches ninety or even eighty, there must be 100,000 who have been carried to their graves. Moreover, none of them really had much of a life anyway. What earthly good is just settin' and loafin' and not even thinkin'? Better you die early, and make room for people who are eager to *live*! Live joyfully and with great zest.

The latter pattern requires that you do exercise. For instance, it is now known that reasonably *hard* physical exercise, done regularly over the years, is the best insurance against heart attack. Just check into the backgrounds of those stooped, wobbly, trembly old men and women who may be no more than sixty years of age. Almost invariably, they have been physical goof-offs, loafers. This is not a put-down for them; perhaps many are burdened with poor body chemistry which precludes much exercise. On the other hand (say the medical theoreticians) probably if they had forced themselves to jog and work in the garden and swim and take walks their body chemistry would have adjusted to proper health level.

Ten good books could be written about how you should exercise. Probably 10,000 already have been written. And you don't really need any of them. First off—go to any reputable physician for a complete physical checkup, including heart, lungs, blood pressure, everything. Then, with him, set up a personal regimen.

Shall I do a lot of walking? Jogging? How much each day?

Now that I'm old, shall I climb stairs?

What about golf? Gardening with its stooping and lifting? Swimming? Dancing? Shuffleboard? Bowling?

It is presumptuous and dangerous for any friend to tell you how to exercise. Each one of us is an individual case; your needs in physical exertion may be quite different from mine, and either one of us could kill himself by foolishly imitating the other. My good friend Lyle Busick jogs five miles every morning, except on Fridays when he and a club of friends all walk about twenty-five miles. He also swims after he jogs. Growing toward eighty, he is the picture of health. In fact, one day when three teenaged boys grabbed his wife's purse in downtown Laguna Beach and ran with it, Lyle jumped out of his car, gave chase, ran them half a mile up the canyon, caught them exhausted and panting, and stood over them until the police arrived. Poetic justice! The newspapers honored Lyle with an article and photos for that feat. (In the swimming pool, we now call him a "snatcher catcher"!)

But Lyle has *been* walking and jogging—for years. If you jogged five miles today, for the first time, we'd probably have to bury you.

So do use a bit of common sense. Don't take my counsel or anybody else's about what kind of exercise and how much of it to get; take your physician's.

⟦ SEEING TWO PRETTY GIRLS ⟧
⟦ WHEN ONLY ONE IS THERE ⟧

If you can "see as well as you ever did," which is unlikely no matter what you may think, you are one in a thousand among us seniors. Our modern society tragically mistreats its eyes.

Good friend Paul Case got me into his office, spent an hour with his nurse helping in a thorough checkup of my eyes. Then he said to me, "You are okay for now. But when you see two pretty girls standing yonder on the corner, or two moons together in the sky, come back to me at once." I was barely forty then. At the age of fifty-one I saw the two girls, and when I got there she wasn't even pretty. I also saw two moons, overlapping. Paul put glasses on me; he said they gave me an air of distinction—the bum. Glasses are an abomination, a nuisance, just as hearing aids are. They are crutches. Nevertheless—thank God for all such helps. The human species is millions of years old, but has had eyeglasses barely two centuries. Wasn't it Ben Franklin who thought up the first bifocals? Well, anyway, dispense with your vanity and wear glasses if you need them; and let an *ophthalmologist* decide when.

In our society too many people are called "doctor." The term can be very misleading. So—genial, handsome Dr. Bill Zarhigh, who charges outrageously and advertises similarly, may be completely incompetent to determine the health status of your eyes. This is not to say that *all* optometrists and oculists are suspect; indeed most are honest and earnest. But they are not trained physicians, they are only fitters of eyeglasses, incapable of any real depth study or of doing surgery which is often needed on elderly folks' eyes, such as removal of cataracts. But the ophthalmologist *is* a physician, highly trained as an eye specialist. The ophthalmologist *can* prescribe your glasses with complete safety for you, as well as keep alert to any disease or other deterioration in your eyes.

If you wear glasses in early "old" age (forty to sixty) an eye test every two or three years may be sufficient. From the age of sixty up—every year is best. In any case, let the ophthalmologist say how often, and pay no attention to your friends or your own impulses. Keep in mind that eyesight is much too precious for carelesssess or gambling.

⟦ HAIR TODAY GONE TOMORROW ⟧

No sir, there is no preventive, absolutely no "cure," for baldness. Ignore all promises about that from barbers or patent-lotion peddlers. Barbers can cut hair. Most are honest, friendly citizens. But no one is able to prevent baldness or restore hair after you are bald, no matter what kind of tonic or goop he offers to sell you.

The same is true of graying hair. Except in rare instances.

But neither baldness nor gray hair is a catastrophe, except to our vanities. Your cue, sir or madam, is simply to grin-and-bear-it and waste no money on "cures." Let your sense of humor and your sense of proportion dictate your actions here.

If you wish, you can buy very fine, fashionable, becoming wigs or hairpieces, for either sex. These coverups, once sneered at and even held to be slightly sinful, now have complete social approval everywhere—which is a blessing. For people much in the public eye, such as actors, politicians and salespersons, hairpieces can have a definite advantage. The good ones are rather costly, and any of them has disadvantages in terms of care and comfort. A hairpiece can be very hot in summer. On the other hand, it can be delightfully protective in winter's cold, and it surely does improve your looks any time.

But for you aging ladies and gentlemen—what's wrong with just being gray-haired? Many of the handsomest people on earth have gray or even white hair. Remember the "silver-tongued" orator? He also had silver hair. *Any* pimply, immature youth, aged six to fifty or so, can have black hair or red hair. But silver hair is ipso facto a proclamation of maturity. At least it says you are *old* enough to act sensibly; whether you do or not is another problem. Gray hair makes a good impression. With it, you can look wise, even when you are merely silent!

86

Because of fashion demands women need wigs more than men. Women also need hair dyes more than men. There's something pitiful, childish, about an old gent of seventy or so who "touches up" his hair with black goo every few days, straining to look young. Why not just be proud that you have lived to be seventy, Buster, and go forth with silver locks waving happily in the breeze? The younger ladies will still admire you— I guarantee it!

Hair health? Baldness and graying are never fatal. Spend minimum money on advertised "shampoos" and "restoratives" and "conditioners" and "rinses" and all that poppycock. Remember—yours is the age of wisdom.

⟦ YOUR DIGESTION ⟧
OR LACK OF IT

"I spent fifty years earning enough money to buy gourmet viands, and now I have to live on milk and crackers."

The old saw is not funny. Because it is all too often a fact of elderly life. You strained to get rich; what you got was—ulcers. Digestion—*in*digestion—ranks close to the top on the list of worries nursed by us old people. It is even associated with that matter discussed in chapter one—our departure from earth. My stomach hurts me so much, so chronically, I very probably will die real soon now.

But if your stomach aches, it may not really be your stomach at all. It may be some disturbance in your colon many feet away. It may possibly be due to incipient appendicitis. Or perhaps your "acid stomach" is

87

caused by—what? Maybe by trying to gobble every kind of food in sight, like a teenager. Can you see your toes just by dropping your chin and not leaning forward? The obese old gent or old lady is all too common; some of us are so enormous as to be shocking. Also many of us skinny ones have stomachaches.

Well, in any case, please don't dose yourself.

True, you have seen a shapely young thing come onto the TV screen with precisely the dosage you need. She herself says so. "More doctors recommend this medicine than any other," she assures you in melodious cow-mooing tones. She may even be in nurse's costume, and appear to be standing in a laboratory; which of course proves that she is eminently qualified to prescribe for you—right?

Wrong. More often than not, the concoction she sells is primarily alcohol with a mess of vitamin B in it, so the reputable physicians declare. Cost of producing it may total as high as seventeen cents. Cost to you may reach up to five dollars. *Benefit* to you may be measurable at minus zero, even though she coos that "I have to take care of the family I love, so to maintain my good health I take Bleep ev-ry day."

An hour later, she is replaced by a curly-haired Greek-god type who adorns the screen with professional mannerisms and slyly suggests that "irregularity can be a problem for any of us, but if you take these pills . . . this pleasant elixir . . . this simple formula. . . ." On and on, ad nauseam. Literally.

Repeat: Let your qualified doctor do the prescribing, friends; not some slick advertising salesperson. Go in for a regular health checkup. Tell him *all*, everything about your interior processes. Then do precisely what he says.

⟦The Too-Common Cold⟧

Very soon this abominable ailment may be eradicated from the face of the earth. Even as I write this, the morning paper tells of a new biochemical called "transfer factor" which shows great promise in fighting viruses, bacteria, and fungus infections, including even leprosy and cancer. At the moment, it is a crumb of hope. Give those research technicians a little more time and, God willing——

The cold-in-the-head is a virus thing, for which there is currently no positively known preventive or cure. (Possibly by the time you read this we'll have it—we live in hope.) Therefore do not dose yourself with advertised nostrums. Your doctor will recommend a few things that may make you more comfortable if you have a cold. So listen to him.

One popular fad today is a heavy intake of vitamin C; from 250 to 750 milligrams per day, both as a cold preventive and cure. That vitamin C dosage, strangely enough, seems to have many qualified advocates, who have conducted extensive tests with results that are downright exciting. Doctors themselves are divided in their opinions about it, hence we ordinary folk are in a quandary. There is one consolation: your doctor probably will let you *try* vitamin C, regardless. Its intake generally is held to be harmless, and might really do you some good. No, I am not prescribing, just reporting. Ask the doc you trust.

Another new discovery about colds, quite revolutionary:

Recent extensive research is said to have proved that sneezing does not spread the cold virus—never. You just don't sneeze out the cold viruses—don't ask me why. So do not be alarmed if some cluck sneezes near you in a crowded bus.

How, then?

They say (you know "they," the people who are responsible for everything) that the virus is spread only by physical contact. Thus if you handle a teacup, plate, silverware, towel, washrag or other item first handled by a person with a head cold—look out! Colds are thus highly infectious. Never kiss the sweet baby who has a cold; sterilize him instead, and isolate him from the rest of the family as much as possible. Isolate careless old Grandpop, too, dang his lovable soul! *Do not touch anything a person with a cold has handled*, until it is sterilized.

Finally—never mind about shutting all the windows up tight. "Don't go outdoors in the chill, you'll catch cold." No such thing. The authorities now know for sure that low temperature in the air has no relation whatsoever to a cold in the head. Which is a bit comforting, isn't it? As well as a bit upsetting to us who are so wedded to folklore.

⟦ TRIPPING, SLIPPING, AND FALLING ⟧

Of all the day-to-day dangers that we really old men and women face, falling seems to rank first.

For many of us, especially those past seventy-five,

the fear of falling and becoming bedridden or, at best, relegated to a wheelchair, is almost obsessive.

It is a justifiable fear. We oldsters do tend to fall, through no real fault of our own. Falling is a definite dragon in our path of life. In fact I'd rather meet a fire-snorting reptile twenty feet long than fall down our flight of sixteen stairs. I could take down my old army sword and slash off that booger's scaly head, and get my picture in the papers for doing so. But if I fall down the stupid steps and break my neck, back, leg, wrist, shoulder, ribs, cranium, or any combination thereof——

Most of our falls in old age are, flatly, due to inattention—plain old carelessness. We *know* our eyesight is not as good as it once was; we *know* that our reflexes are nowhere near as good as they were twenty years or so ago. Yet we barge along, our minds in the clouds, as if we were seventeen instead of seventy.

Old eyes often just can't see the six-inch step-down in the hallway or sidewalk. They do not see the protruding rock or root, the hiked-up rug or the slippery floor—why in heaven's name does any housewife of any age ever insist on polishing her floors to ice-rink slipperiness anyway? So, we trip and break a hip. Or worse.

[[CAUTION! OLD PEOPLE WALKING]]

There is, of course, no prevention for those disasters except to move with constant, extra caution. Because our reflexes are no longer fast, we are likely not to catch ourselves with our hands if we trip. Our aging bones are more brittle, hence more likely to break. They also take much longer to heal than they did in our youth.

Knowing these dangers, move always with studied care. Be especially wary of wet floors and bathtubs. It has been established that the bathroom is the most dangerous part of any home for any person, certainly for Grandmother and Grandfather. Tubs are made preposterously slick and dangerous, quite unnecessarily. But there are inexpensive, strongly adhesive, rough topped stickers that you can buy and apply permanently to the bottom of your bathtub or your shower bath. They are even ornamental. Your feet do not slide over them; you are unlikely to slip at all when they are beneath you. Get them at your plumber's, or for less money at almost any novelty store, department store, or discount house. But get them, for sure.

"I Remember Your Face, Old Friend, But . . ."

Do not feel embarrassed. It happens to us all. Every day. Pardon me, sir, I do know that we went to school together and have been in the same Kiwanis Club for the past twenty-eight years, but at the moment I just can't recall your name. Ah, me.

Think nothing of it if you, too, sometimes wind the cat and put the clock out the door at bedtime, figuratively. *You are not sick.* Your brain is not deteriorating —much. All of us are absent-minded. This annoying trait is most common among so-called intellectuals, even those as young as 30.

So smile about it, laugh with your family and friends, and just try to keep your mind exercised and alert.

That peculiar quirk is definitely not something critical, no matter how put out you feel with yourself when you lock the car keys in the car. The cause may be poor blood pressure or circulation, may be lack of exercise, may be changing body chemistry—who knows? Best course is just to swap such experiences with friends over a cup of coffee. Tell them:

"There are only three things I forget. I forget names. I forget faces—And I forget what the third one is."

"I Did Not Sleep a Wink Last Night—I Swear It!"

Don't swear; that's vulgar. And anyway, the truth is that you did sleep several hours in spite of what you think and how you feel here at breakfast. The phenomenon is as common as morning coffee and toast.

Insomnia, of course, is very real. It is an abomination which, as with absent-mindedness, can strike persons of any age. Again, it seems to prefer people with very active, intelligent minds, especially senior citizens. The dumb cluck, the clod—forgive the slang—usually just goes to bed and conks out all night. We can envy him that.

If your sleeplessness is a new thing and seems acute, consult your doctor. But do not be alarmed; virtually nobody has ever died from it, or even suffered lasting ill effects.

Most of us do not need as much sleep as we think we do anyway. We have tended to make eight hours of sleep almost a sacred requirement, whereas millions of happy folk sleep only six or seven hours, some less than that. The extroverts—gregarious, outgoing types—require less than the introverted "deep thinkers" who are less social-minded. Even you and your mate may have a two-hour variance in sleep need.

Authorities in this field also declare that habit patterns formed in childhood can carry over and have an effect in old age, especially in your time of awakening and arising for the day. Many of us oldsters were reared on farms where we had to arise at four or five A.M. and get the morning chores done before breakfast so that field work could start with the rising sun. I was such a farmer. And to this day I am still up before the sun, and enjoy the dawn. But my Adele was a city girl who "slept in." Today she goes to bed after I do, and gets up after I do. Invariably we awake about three A.M. for a trip to the bathroom, then lie awake for an hour or more talking, or just thinking. Then if in the middle of the morning or middle of the afternoon we feel like taking a siesta, we take it. Maybe we are geniuses! A genius named Thomas Edison slept only three or four hours a night, but might take three or four sudden naps during the day if he felt the urge.

Take absolutely no sleeping pills or potions, unless they are prescribed by your doctor (not some family member or friend). Even then, make any use of them short-term. Especially should you avoid the advertised sleep medicines because all of them can be addictive in some measure, and they may do you more harm than good.

All factors considered, the authorities agree, the best way to prevent or end insomnia is to revise and upgrade your habit patterns, your mental and emotional attitudes. No childish "counting of sheep" is going to help you. You are a mature person; so simply say your prayers and then "let go" mentally.

⟦ Skin Problems ⟧

I have a plague of them—endless little lesions and pimples and scaly places and red spots and brown spots, some that bleed and some that don't, some that soon go away and others that linger so as to require burning or freezing off or even X-ray treatments. I have had three malignancies which, if neglected, might well have killed me.

In varying degrees, such phenomena are almost universal among aging folk, especially men. Most of them are attributed to too much sunshine—yes, the same glorious sunshine which we tend to worship because it brightens our spirits. We grew up in an era when it was fashionable to loll around near-naked in the sun. We thought that a tan made us handsome or beautiful and healthy. It didn't; the actinic rays of the sun simply started skin problems. Many of us of course had to work in the sun, and we too have paid a price. You can issue a warning now to your young grandchildren about deliberately taking too much sunshine—not that they will accept it! Skin problems are far worse in the gloriously sunny Southwest than in gloomily overcast England and New England. Throughout Texas, New Mexico, Arizona, California, Nevada, Oklahoma, you can encounter thousands of old geezers with unsightly bleedy little sores on faces and necks, despite their abiding tan.

95

If your skin shows *any* type of sores, bleeding spots, swellings, or scalings, that persist longer than a month, go at once to a reputable dermatologist. Be guided by the wisdom of a real skin specialist.

And what about wrinkles?

Cherish them!

Be grateful; you have lived long enough to have them. You can't escape them, nor get rid of them, and straining to cover them up with drugstore goo merely makes you look silly, so smile and be proud of them. They are marks of venerability and—let us hope—wisdom. After all, most of us millions over the age of sixty have wrinkles, so we can call them our badge of distinction. Come to think of it, whoever said that wrinkles aren't beautiful anyway? God puts ripple-wrinkles on the drifting sand dunes, and certainly on the surfaces of his magnificent forest lakes. Why not let them beautify us old geezers and gals?

⟦ AND NOW, AT LONG LAST, THE "BIG" PROBLEM— ⟧
⟦ "WHAT ABOUT MY WEIGHT?" ⟧

Virtually every magazine and newspaper you pick up has fabulous articles and advertisements about weight control. Also there are endless books on this subject.

Promises, promises; talk, talk! Far, far more is being said about weight control than is being done about it.

Friends, please do not *talk* about your weight.

The self-pitying, sympathy-seeking diet faddists have become an abomination on the scene. They bore the

96

bejabbers out of everybody who is forced to listen. All too often we aging folk head that parade.

Many try to rationalize their overeating habits by saying they "inherited the tendency" toward obesity. Maybe they did, in some small measure. But generally— no! A few doctors do tell neurotic patients that the tendency to get fat came from their parents, but that's largely hogwash. *People get fat because they stuff food into their mouths*. When we try to "make fun of it" we are simply advertising our lack of willpower and seeking sympathy we do not deserve.

So—what's to be done?

Just one case history will answer the question for you: a gentleman in Costa Mesa—weighing in at 254 pounds with a height of only five-feet-five—came to grips with himself. He told himself and his family, "I am eating emotionally. I eat when I am happy, I eat when I am unhappy. This is ridiculous. What I need is not a fad 'diet' but to change my eating habits, permanently."

In forty weeks he dropped 100 pounds. He is now a happy jogger-golfer.

Exercise played no role in his weight loss. For the average person, exercise is an overrated tool in weight reduction. It is better to lose weight first, then begin an exercise program, starting mildly and increasing gradually. There are exceptions: my Adele's doctor prescribed half a mile of swimming each day plus a mile of walking plus a very restricted diet for six months; it became a pleasant regimen in which she dropped from

158 pounds to 134—and lost her arthritis pains as a bonus. Oh sure, it took some willpower. But what worthwhile achievement doesn't? A year later, Adele was still "*slim* and sassy."

So it can be done. Just don't delude yourself by saying that you are "stout" when your belly bulges. Friend, you are *fat*. Too fat. Start a weight-reduction program at once—by going first to your reputable physician, then doing exactly what he says. Don't talk, act!

WE SKINNY ONES DEMAND SYMPATHY TOO

You slobs outnumber us. Seven out of every ten people in most neighborhoods are *over*weight.

But we three remaining ones are crybabies, too. Give us an opening any time anywhere and we will tell you how much we strive to "build ourselves up" with scant success. And what do you do? You glare at us! Only last week I went to one of these modern, you know, hot-bath jacuzzi pools in a health club. Useless things, costly to join, but faddish at the moment. Sitting down there in the water were seven fellows each weighing more than 200 pounds. There on the tiled step stood I, a beanpole at 134 pounds. They were all friends of mine, but they all glared at me and one said to the others, "Let's drown him."

All right, we gentlefolk do try to laugh at our problems, and good-humored living is indeed imperative. But at a height of six feet, my massive 134 pounds means I have limited energies, I have "nerves," and assorted imaginary ills and traumas. We skinny types force-feed ourselves, but get a little sick from it. Maybe we are lucky? Maybe we are. But we nurse envy for you stout folk.

If you are one of us skinnies—again do not diet without a physician's guidance. Do not leap at advertised food supplements and other gimmicks. "Every body needs milk," the TV and other advertising media shout at us all, over and over every day, adding that every citizen needs a quart of cow milk a day to be healthy. Don't you believe it! Milk is a wholesome food, yes; so if you like the slimy stuff, drink it. But it is no more imperative for us than are bananas, or yogurt, or spinach, or any of a hundred other "health" foods. Three-fourths of the world never heard of drinking cow milk, don't even know what a cow looks like. Nature provided for human beings to have human milk for their first few months of life, then no other milk unless desired. So do not be panicked by propaganda from the dairy lobby. It's the same with butter; good quality margarine is just as nourishing, and far less expensive. On the other hand, dairy products can make some of us skinny ones gain a few pounds; but most likely we won't hold them long. Our body chemistry just isn't geared to holding much additional weight. So say the best authorities.

Thus it is that you heavies are more fortunate; you *can* reduce, and stay down. It is almost impossible for us skinnies to put weight on and hold it; straining at it, we get sickish.

If you are fat, don't fret; just quietly take action.

If you are lean, don't fret; just restrict your energy

output to match your intake, get ample rest, and culti-
vate a calm attitude.

None of us can afford to "weigh" either problem
unduly. In fact that's true no matter what your health
difficulty may be.

7.

Your Old-Age Personality

Now here is a chapter topic that is far and away the most *important* in this book.

Yet, strangely, the subject ranks close to zero on the scale of old people's consideration. We are deeply concerned (as has been shown) about approaching death, about the antics of young people, about the accelerating rate of change in our lives, about money, about health. But we rarely think about our personality projections at all. Each of us seems tacitly to assume that his or her personality, though perhaps not perfect, could not be improved. You may think of yours as being "just right."

Well, I have news for you: it isn't.

Almost certainly, if you have passed the age of fifty-five or so you have become a trifle hidebound, opinionated, authoritarian, inflexible, crotchety, touchy, sensitive, bossy, demanding—some of those or all of them—and *without realizing it*.

If you haven't, you may indeed be "a gem of purest ray serene," but I doubt it. Oh yes, I have met quite a few men and women who appear to have mellowed in old age. The kinsman or friend who drops in only for an occasional visit usually calls them "sweet" or "gentle" or even "darling," as if they were little children, these dear, dear old ones.

In point of fact, most of them are simply dullards.

They are likely to be men or women who have retreated from life; who have reached "acceptance," or "resignation to the inevitable," or some such nonsense. They simply try to smile at every caller and appear lovable.

Nuts to them. I'd rather see Grandpappy get bitin' mad because he missed a two-foot putt. I'd rather see him throw his paper down in disgust because of some political shenanigans out of the nation's capital. I would rather hear him (as I did overhear one grand old fellow) say emphatically to his sixteen-year-old grandson, "You are a damn fool if you take up smoking. Now throw that stinking cigarette away, come over here and let me tell you how to *really* impress your gang and the girls, and yourself." The boy and his two sisters all sat cross-legged on the lawn grass with him, and listened. He minced no words, though he spoke kindly. Incidentally, the boy never smoked again. And those kids all but worship Grandpop.

Or consider Grandmother.

Now *there's* a character in American tradition! The archetype is pictured by artists and poets and silly essayists and sentimentalists as being the very essence of sweetness and helplessness.

But that's pure corn. Saccharine. She is not really like that, and never was. Away back yonder, she toted the rifle and drove the mules, held enemies at bay and sassed the preacher, and kept her family in line until they buried her. Today, she is not quite as admirable, maybe, because she plays too much bridge, gallivants too much, eats too much, and hence weighs too much, and tends to have firmly set lips that are ever ready—not to mention able—to tell the Chief Executive how to run the country.

Well, greetings, Grandmom!

Welcome to our church and our clubs and our excitements, welcome to our homes and our lives. We love you. But we wouldn't, if you were a mealy-mouthed, self-pitying old blob of fat who just waddled around and criticized. Even so, you are not perfect, no more than Grandpop is. And you both will get worse, if you don't take yourselves firmly in hand, immediately.

⟦ POOR HEALTH ⟧
⟦ POOR PERSONALITY ⟧

Poor health is bad enough. But in its effect on your overall success in living, your happiness, your peace of mind, a poor personality is infinitely worse. The two are closely related.

Many people are unwell, lacking in energy and zest. In fact it has been said that 90 percent of the world's work is being done by people who don't feel very well this morning. Yet somehow the vast majority of these people manage to maintain good spirits. They get along with their families, their business associates, and the strangers they encounter. They hum and whistle and smile, even when the back aches and the arm is stiff. They remain in *control*, quietly determined to enjoy life, regardless. Magnificent Abraham Lincoln reminded us that "people are about as happy as they make up their minds to be."

Tragically, too many of us wrinkled ones do not make up our minds to have happy personalities.

We lack the spiritual undergirding that comes only from a closeness with God. If, in some fancied sophistication, you sneer or smile loftily at that statement, your conceit will wreck all your remaining days on earth. Any genuine happiness has to begin with humility.

Humility is not by any means the same as meekness. Humility is saying that without God's guidance you can accomplish nothing; that of yourself you have no strength, no control, and can only wave with the winds. But with divine guidance, not even a figurative cyclone can harm you. By contrast, self-denigrating meekness means a complete washout of personality. It's not the "meek" who shall inherit the earth, but the humble who are spiritually strong. That's what the word "meek" meant when that famous promise of Jesus was first written in English; today its meaning is quite different.

Humility—faith in God—is what will enable you to triumph over poor physical health. Even if the ailment can never be cured, the spiritually strong person can triumph. We have all witnessed just that, dozens of times. But for too many millions of us, poor physical health brings on a quavering fear—which of course means that the total personality is then at low, low ebb. Physical and mental illness can go hand in hand, and only a strong spiritual undergirding can prevent total deterioration.

⟦Senility⟧

Senility is a horrifying phenomenon which society commonly associates with old age and poor health. It is a tragic condition which reveals a deterioration of the mind that makes us act and feel foolish, fanciful, childish, with thoughts wandering, memory failing, and judgment impaired. We are just lucid enough to know that we are pitiful and dependent, and therefore we are deeply depressed. We see that we are laughed at, mocked, and ridiculed as "silly."

Well, old friends—take heart.

I have good news for you! Do not berate yourselves. Do not accuse yourselves of having forgotten God, of sinning.

Until recently, the condition called senility was generally attributed to arteriosclerosis, the medical term for hardening of the arteries. That hardening was thought to be caused by a buildup of cholesterol and calcium which clogged the blood vessels, thereby cutting down on the blood flow, which in turn lowered the brain's supply of oxygen, causing it to function very poorly. There seemed to be little or no way to prevent such a condition, which was caused partly by inheritance anyway. "Hardening of the arteries" became a common fear-phrase in every retirement center and home.

But in the early 1970s, scientists completed new, intense studies into the matter. The results are very important, very heartening.

These studies revealed that senility is due mainly to *a sudden cessation of most mental activity and gym-*

nastics such as occurs when we retire or stop active work.

Another way of expressing it is—the brain can never be allowed to retire. The body, maybe; in some measure it can edge off. The brain—no.

Senility is now known to be tied directly to a reduction of mental stimulation, and the withdrawal from society and reality that often accompanies physical aging. Therefore it is preventable, and the prevention technique can be very pleasant.

In a word—don't stop thinking.

Do not let your mind atrophy or get flabby from lack of use, as your muscles do if you stop using them. Lie in bed for a few months, taking virtually no physical exercise, and your body will be a weakened mess! Usually, such a mistreated body can be rebuilt. A weakening of the mind is much more difficult to reverse; it usually just slides on downhill.

It is barely necessary to repeat that the personality of the senile one is subzero. The tragedy is that the victim himself knows that, and can do nothing about it. So, in heaven's name——

⟦ Prevention! ⟧

Whenever you retire or otherwise begin to ease off from life's normal stimulations for the mind, take yourself in hand. Seek new outlets immediately, new mental horizons. Read new things; you will be astounded at what a world of pleasure and benefit is to be found in books, not just the stuffy old "classics" but current books, both fact and fiction. No, no, no, despite the headlines and the word-of-mouth noise about them, books today are *not* all pornographic, filled with trashy sex and violence. Actually, *religious* books (commentaries, personal and family guidance, inspirational works of all kinds, in addition to new translations of the Bible) are selling at an all-time high. Similarly, not everything on television is "thin" in value. That magic box can be a treasure for the mind, if you make yourself selective in choosing programs.

Go places, if you can. Join discussion groups. Meet old friends, yes, but by all means meet new people too. Talk some, but listen more. Get a little angry now an then, as at social injustices, and at crooked politicians; sound off about them, and to them.

Take a new, rededicated, and very active part in your church. Don't just doze in your pew "because you are old." Invite the minister to your home for dinner, discuss the sermon, talk about the total programming of the church or synagogue, about how you and your mate can help in the uplift of humanity. Such an approach to life is unbelievably exalting, invigorating, healing, stimulating; it's an absolute guarantee against senility.

Write letters. Not whining, self-pitying pleas for sympathy, but encouraging, appreciative messages to your younger kin and friends who are still fighting life's battles. Remember that the strongest magic you can use in dealing with other people is a simple compliment; a word of commendation, an encouragement. That statement comes not from me, an oldster like yourself; it comes from a man of faith who is possibly the most famous psychologist in America today, another gray-haired gentleman, George W. Crane. He *knows* people, especially us older ones; knows what motivates us, what can keep us alert and happy and totally alive.

To prevent senility, never let yourself sit down and brood. Instead—*do* something! Make speeches. Join committees. Sound off. Not mere "entertainment," not self-pampering "recreation" which many oldsters feel impelled to pursue, saying they have earned it. That's self-delusion. We see such types by the thousands, typically on cruise ships; the rich set, running, hiding from themselves or trying to hide, pursuing an impossible "happiness" by gambling, drinking, carousing, mistreating both body and mind. Follow through on almost any group of them, and you'll find that a pitiful mental state develops all too soon. Call it senility, call it illness, call it what you will. It has been brought on by a frantic, fear-ridden straining to escape—from what? Superficiality. Boredom. Creative living.

Senility is a complex state caused by more than bloated, brittle blood vessels. The experts now know that the secrets of the senile are locked in the murky inner workings of the mind. Avoiding that condition is an imperative. You will never reveal a personality worth having if you "let your mind run down."

⟦How Mean Are You?⟧

Senility is not the same as meanness.

Meanness, the ugly temper, the crotchety-touchy-sensitive personality, is far more common than senility. It too, of course, stems from a spiritual situation. It proclaims a lack of tenderness, a neglect of that divine concept we call love. This tragic condition can be developed by anybody of *any* age, of course, but the tendency toward it seems to be increased when we turn sixty or so. The crotchety old man or woman is almost a stereotype; a gray-hair with the unsmiling, no-nonsense approach to life. The lips are turned down, or set firmly in a straight line. The eyes glare at other people, especially if the others say or do something that doesn't quite match the oldster's opinion. Such an intolerant person "judges," becomes touchy, cantankerous, supersensitive, snappish in speech, even profane at times. You know the type—all too common on the social scene.

But at the opposite pole are the mellowed men and women who somehow seem forever to exude *warmth*! They show an abiding cheer and goodwill, even when suffering physically, financially, and emotionally at times. Thus they are in command of themselves, they have psychomotor control.

⟦ YOUR ALL-IMPORTANT SENSE OF HUMOR ⟧

In a quick finale, let me suggest that most personality faults can be prevented—or corrected—by consciously developing *a sense of humor*. Virtually all authorities (including most clergy) heartily agree.

This does not mean that you must strain at being "funny" at all times; indeed the compulsive joker is an abomination. A *sense* of humor is a much higher concept than just being a humorist.

A sense of humor means that you react to most of life's annoying little phenomena with smiling goodwill, rather than with touchiness or criticism.

It is closely allied with tenderness, kindness, understanding, sympathy, gentleness, tolerance, forbearance, and love.

Those who have it smile often, chuckle often, and laugh heartily on occasion.

One distinguished psychiatrist, speaking for all his colleagues, says flatly that "a wholesome sense of humor is equal in importance to a wholesome set of morals." It is a priceless secret of happiness available to us all!

8.
Questions and Answers

Aging folk ask many questions of their ministers, doctors, bankers, attorneys and other counselors. Here are those that are heard most often, with answers that have been carefully researched and checked for accuracy:

*What mistakes should we oldsters strive
hardest to avoid?*

Probably the same ones that the great statesman and philosopher, Cicero, listed 2,000 years ago in Rome:

The delusion that personal gain is made by crushing others.

The tendency to worry about things that cannot be changed or corrected.

Insisting that a thing is impossible because we cannot accomplish it.

Refusing to set aside trivial preferences.

Neglecting development and refinement of the mind.

Attempting to compel others to believe as we do.

*What are the most dangerous myths about
old age?*

That all old people are twisted, bent· over, and immobile. (This is the all-to-common but highly distorted stereotype.)

That any person past retirement age has wasted away.

That persons past sixty-five have almost no mental capabilities.

That youth is taking over and we oldsters are being put on the shelf.

That senility is inevitable.

That we should rest long hours every day.

Should we get more sleep when we become old?

Not necessarily. Many virile men and women in their seventies and eighties do fine on six or seven hours. Eight is still standard. New research shows that pattern sleepers share certain personality traits, regardless of age. For instance, short sleepers are more success-oriented, achievement types. Long sleepers tend to be passive, introverted, and depressed.

How can I cure a tendency toward hypochondria?

Take a vow of silence. With determination, set and keep a course of not complaining or even mentioning your symptoms of illness, real or fancied, *for at least six months*. Then go to any reputable physician and tell him every symptom you can think of! When he is through treating you, take another vow of silence for six months, and repeat that process forever.

Usually, hypochondria is merely a put-on plea for sympathy, a technique for getting attention. So refocus your mind.

*What is the main cause of quarrels or coolness
between old couples?*

Self-pity, plus selfishness. The mate "owes" you
nothing that you don't owe the mate. True love is an
outreach, not an intake.

*Is prayer important for old people, in this
modern sophisticated era?*

What a stupid question!

Certainly it is important. "Sophistication" is based
on sophistry, or false reasoning. It is put-on, pose, un-
realistic, self-deluding. Prayer is more important today
than ever before, for persons of all ages. Prayer is vital
to your very soul; group prayer, as in the worshiping
community, and private prayer, such as when you talk
to God—and listen to him!—while in your bed, or when
you walk beside the sea or sit on a park bench alone.

How often should I go to my analyst?

What analyst? Who is he? What does he "analyze"?

Parlor psychiatry is a national fad; and millions of
dollars are wasted on "analysts." To be sure, there is
a plague of genuine mental illness, and victims do need
expert clinical help. But that doesn't authorize you to
trot to some hoked-up "expert" recommended by a
flighty friend. If you are truly disturbed, ask your physician to recommend a reputable psychiatrist. But remember—one of the latter (William Bede McGrath,
author of the book *Mental Fitness*) has said that
"Eighty percent of all the mental illness that comes
before me could have been prevented, or could yet be
cured, *by simple kindness.*"

113

Take that to heart. Also, see the answer to the question above this one.

How can I safely reduce my weight?
Guided by a reputable doctor, cut down on your food intake. That is the *only* approved way. Ignore all fad diets. Avoid all advertised pills, potions, and courses of exercise.

I get so bored with television. What shall I do?
Turn the thing off!

Walk away from it. Center your major attention and energies on more constructive outlets such as craft work (sewing, ceramics, wood carvings, carpentry, rock sculpture, leather tooling), new courses in reading, service at your church, volunteer work, gardening, swimming, attending lectures, taking college courses—heavens, there is no end to the wonderful things you can do beside glue your eyes to that TV screen.

On the other hand, TV has some merit. So, pick and choose. At breakfast table, make a quick list of the programs that you feel will be worthy for entertainment or information—maybe three to four hours a day, average.

So many of us oldsters are "singles." How can we find mates for marriage?
The old maid, the old bachelor, the widow, the widower, are indeed prominent among people past sixty or so. Of course, many have the good judgment and good fortune to start courtships on their own. But far more of their kind do not.

114

Therefore—take heart.

Sit down at once and write a simple note to: Scientific Marriage Foundation, Hopkins Building, Mellott, Indiana. Just say "Please send me information about your service," then list your name and address. Men applicants especially are urged to write.

Very soon, in a plain envelope that protects your privacy, you will receive instructions. At no time will you be obligated, in any manner. If you are of good character, you may soon be introduced to a potential mate.

Unlike dozens of "come-on" marriage bureaus seeking only your money, this SMF is completely honest and high-level. On its board of control are several of America's foremost clergy and sociologists such as Norman Vincent Peale, George W. Crane, Baptist and Methodist and Presbyterian ministers of national fame, Catholic leaders, Jewish leaders, and well-known philanthropists. It is a strictly nonprofit, in fact a great humanitarian service that has helped thousands of singles (of all ages) get married. Among them, the divorce rate has been less than 1 percent!

We are often told not to talk about our younger years and pleasures, not to reminisce. But why isn't that all right?

It *is* all right. It is pleasant, harmless, wonderful, if you don't develop that habit of living in the past or wallowing in sentimentality. If you insist that *your* day was better than the present, you will be tagged— properly—as an insufferable old bore.

But do get your gang together frequently and share

115

the good memories of yesteryear. By all means speak of your adventures to your modern hepcat grandchildren —if you can get them to listen! They can enjoy it, and learn much. But storytelling (*true* story) is something of an art. Don't labor your reminiscing, don't overdo. Here too good humor is a vital part of success.

Which church should I belong to?

Hah! You are not going to trap me with that one! I'd get 10,000 indignant letters. The answer is as individual as deciding which girl or boy to marry. I think it is best given in this wonderful old story:

Ten farmers were sitting and talking in front of a country store. They got to arguing about the merits of various church organizations. Every man had an emphatic opinion—except old Granddad Weaver. He just sat quietly whittling and listening. Finally the others asked him which church was best.

"Well now," replied he, "there are four roads from this store to the cotton gin. But when you get there, the ginner ain't going to ask you which road you took. He's going to ask, 'How good is your cotton?'"

Which church should you belong to? I won't say *which*. I will say *belong*—and participate. It can be the most meaningful involvement you'll have, in old age or any other age—meaningful for you and for everybody about you.

You know, I really "cotton" to people like you who can stick with me as long as you have. See you in church!